50 Delicious Soup Recipes for Home

By: Kelly Johnson

Table of Contents

- Chicken Noodle Soup
- Tomato Basil Soup
- Butternut Squash Soup
- French Onion Soup
- Minestrone Soup
- Lentil Soup
- Potato Leek Soup
- Split Pea Soup
- Creamy Mushroom Soup
- Thai Coconut Soup (Tom Kha Gai)
- Gazpacho
- Beef Stew Soup
- Clam Chowder
- Corn Chowder
- Borscht (Beet Soup)
- Tortilla Soup
- Ramen Soup
- Chicken Tortilla Soup
- Italian Wedding Soup
- Avgolemono (Greek Lemon Chicken Soup)
- Miso Soup
- Pho (Vietnamese Noodle Soup)
- Moroccan Harira Soup
- Pumpkin Soup
- Wonton Soup
- Cream of Broccoli Soup
- Fish Chowder
- Egg Drop Soup
- Vichyssoise (Cold Potato Leek Soup)
- Sopa de Lima (Mexican Lime Soup)
- Cuban Black Bean Soup
- Sopa de Ajo (Spanish Garlic Soup)
- Hot and Sour Soup
- New England Clam Chowder
- Creamy Cauliflower Soup

- Jamaican Chicken Soup
- Mushroom Barley Soup
- Turkey Chili Soup
- Creamy Tomato Tortellini Soup
- Cabbage Soup
- Malaysian Laksa Soup
- Escarole Soup
- Irish Potato Soup
- Swiss Chard Soup
- Chicken and Rice Soup
- Chicken Mulligatawny Soup
- Japanese Clear Soup
- Corn and Crab Chowder
- Portuguese Caldo Verde
- Hungarian Goulash Soup

Chicken Noodle Soup

Ingredients:

- 1 tablespoon olive oil
- 1 onion, diced
- 2 carrots, sliced
- 2 celery stalks, sliced
- 2 cloves garlic, minced
- 6 cups chicken broth
- 2 cups cooked chicken, shredded or diced
- 1 cup egg noodles (or any noodles of your choice)
- 1 teaspoon dried thyme
- Salt and pepper to taste
- Fresh parsley, chopped (for garnish, optional)

Instructions:

1. Sauté Vegetables: In a large pot or Dutch oven, heat olive oil over medium heat. Add diced onion, carrots, and celery. Sauté for about 5 minutes, until vegetables are softened.
2. Add Garlic and Herbs: Add minced garlic and dried thyme to the pot. Sauté for another minute until fragrant.
3. Add Broth: Pour in chicken broth and bring to a boil. Reduce heat to low and let it simmer for about 10 minutes, allowing the flavors to meld together.
4. Cook Noodles: Add egg noodles to the pot and cook according to package instructions until noodles are tender. This usually takes about 8-10 minutes depending on the type of noodles you use.
5. Add Chicken: Stir in cooked chicken into the soup. If using raw chicken, you can add it earlier with the vegetables and cook until no longer pink.
6. Season: Season with salt and pepper to taste. Adjust seasoning as needed.
7. Serve: Ladle the chicken noodle soup into bowls. Garnish with chopped fresh parsley if desired. Serve hot and enjoy!

This recipe is versatile, so feel free to customize it by adding other vegetables like peas or spinach, or adjusting the seasonings to suit your taste. It's perfect for warming up on a cold day or comforting you when you're under the weather.

Tomato Basil Soup

Ingredients:

- 2 tablespoons olive oil
- 1 onion, chopped
- 2 cloves garlic, minced
- 2 cans (28 oz each) whole tomatoes
- 1 can (14 oz) diced tomatoes
- 1 tablespoon tomato paste
- 1 teaspoon sugar (optional, to balance acidity)
- 1 teaspoon dried basil (or 1/4 cup fresh basil, chopped)
- 2 cups vegetable or chicken broth
- Salt and pepper to taste
- 1/2 cup heavy cream (optional, for a creamy version)
- Fresh basil leaves, thinly sliced (for garnish, optional)

Instructions:

1. Sauté Onion and Garlic: In a large pot or Dutch oven, heat olive oil over medium heat. Add chopped onion and sauté until softened, about 5 minutes. Add minced garlic and cook for another minute until fragrant.
2. Add Tomatoes and Tomato Paste: Add whole tomatoes (including juices) and diced tomatoes (with their juices) to the pot. Break up the whole tomatoes using a spoon or spatula. Stir in tomato paste and sugar, if using.
3. Simmer: Pour in vegetable or chicken broth. Bring the mixture to a boil, then reduce heat to low and let it simmer uncovered for about 20-25 minutes, stirring occasionally, until the flavors meld together and the tomatoes break down.
4. Blend Soup: Remove the pot from heat. Using an immersion blender directly in the pot, blend the soup until smooth. If you don't have an immersion blender, carefully transfer the soup in batches to a blender and blend until smooth, then return it to the pot.
5. Season and Add Basil: Season the soup with salt and pepper to taste. Stir in dried basil (if using fresh basil, reserve it for garnish).
6. Finish with Cream (optional): For a creamy version, stir in heavy cream and warm the soup gently over low heat until heated through. Do not boil once the cream is added.
7. Serve: Ladle the tomato basil soup into bowls. Garnish with thinly sliced fresh basil leaves if desired. Serve hot and enjoy with crusty bread or a grilled cheese sandwich.

This recipe is straightforward and perfect for showcasing the flavors of ripe tomatoes and fragrant basil. Adjust the seasoning and creaminess level according to your preference. It's sure to be a hit for lunch or a light dinner!

Butternut Squash Soup

Ingredients:

- 1 butternut squash (about 2-3 pounds), peeled, seeded, and diced
- 1 onion, chopped
- 2 cloves garlic, minced
- 2 carrots, peeled and chopped
- 2 tablespoons olive oil or butter
- 4 cups vegetable or chicken broth
- 1 teaspoon dried thyme
- 1/2 teaspoon ground cinnamon
- Salt and pepper, to taste
- 1/2 cup heavy cream (optional, for creamier soup)
- Toasted pumpkin seeds or croutons, for garnish (optional)
- Fresh chopped parsley or thyme, for garnish (optional)

Instructions:

1. Prepare the Butternut Squash: Peel the butternut squash using a vegetable peeler. Cut it in half lengthwise, scoop out the seeds, and then dice the squash into 1-inch cubes.
2. Sauté Vegetables: In a large pot or Dutch oven, heat olive oil or melt butter over medium heat. Add chopped onion, minced garlic, and chopped carrots. Sauté for about 5-7 minutes, until the vegetables begin to soften.
3. Add Squash and Spices: Add the diced butternut squash to the pot along with dried thyme and ground cinnamon. Stir well to combine and sauté for another 5 minutes, allowing the spices to become fragrant.
4. Simmer: Pour in the vegetable or chicken broth. Bring the mixture to a boil, then reduce heat to low. Cover and simmer for about 20-25 minutes, or until the butternut squash is tender and easily pierced with a fork.
5. Blend Soup: Remove the pot from heat. Using an immersion blender directly in the pot, blend the soup until smooth. Alternatively, carefully transfer the soup in batches to a blender and blend until smooth, then return it to the pot.
6. Season and Finish: Season the soup with salt and pepper to taste. If you prefer a creamier soup, stir in heavy cream at this point and warm the soup gently over low heat until heated through.
7. Serve: Ladle the butternut squash soup into bowls. Garnish with toasted pumpkin seeds or croutons for crunch, and fresh chopped parsley or thyme for additional flavor. Serve hot and enjoy!

This recipe is versatile, and you can adjust the thickness by adding more broth or cream to your liking. It's a wonderful way to enjoy the natural sweetness of butternut squash in a comforting bowl of soup.

French Onion Soup

Ingredients:

- 4 large onions, thinly sliced
- 3 tablespoons butter
- 2 tablespoons olive oil
- 1 teaspoon granulated sugar (optional, to help with caramelization)
- 2 cloves garlic, minced
- 1/2 cup dry white wine (optional)
- 6 cups beef broth (or a combination of beef and chicken broth)
- 2 bay leaves
- 1 teaspoon dried thyme (or a few sprigs of fresh thyme)
- Salt and pepper, to taste
- Baguette slices, toasted
- 2 cups shredded Gruyère cheese (or Swiss cheese)
- Fresh chopped parsley, for garnish (optional)

Instructions:

1. Caramelize Onions: In a large pot or Dutch oven, melt butter and olive oil over medium heat. Add thinly sliced onions and cook, stirring occasionally, until they become soft and caramelized, about 30-40 minutes. If using, sprinkle sugar over the onions to help with caramelization.
2. Add Garlic: Add minced garlic to the pot and cook for another 1-2 minutes until fragrant.
3. Deglaze with Wine (optional): Pour in dry white wine to deglaze the pot, scraping up any browned bits from the bottom. Let it cook for a few minutes until the wine has mostly evaporated.
4. Simmer Soup: Add beef broth, bay leaves, and dried thyme to the pot. Bring the mixture to a simmer. Reduce heat to low and let the soup simmer, uncovered, for about 20-30 minutes to allow the flavors to meld together. Season with salt and pepper to taste.
5. Prepare Baguette: While the soup is simmering, preheat your oven's broiler. Arrange baguette slices on a baking sheet and toast them under the broiler until they are golden and crispy on both sides.
6. Assemble and Serve: Discard the bay leaves from the soup. Ladle the hot soup into oven-safe bowls. Place a few toasted baguette slices on top of each bowl, covering the surface of the soup. Sprinkle shredded Gruyère cheese generously over the baguette slices and soup.
7. Broil: Place the bowls on a baking sheet and place them under the broiler. Broil for 2-3 minutes, or until the cheese is melted and bubbly and slightly golden brown.
8. Garnish and Serve: Carefully remove the bowls from the oven. Garnish with fresh chopped parsley if desired. Serve hot and enjoy immediately.

French Onion Soup is best served hot and right out of the oven, with the cheese melted and gooey. It's a comforting and satisfying soup that's perfect for a cozy dinner or a special occasion.

Minestrone Soup

Ingredients:

- 2 tablespoons olive oil
- 1 onion, chopped
- 2 cloves garlic, minced
- 2 carrots, diced
- 2 celery stalks, diced
- 1 zucchini, diced
- 1 yellow squash, diced
- 1 cup green beans, trimmed and cut into bite-sized pieces
- 1 can (14 oz) diced tomatoes (or use fresh tomatoes, chopped)
- 6 cups vegetable broth or chicken broth
- 1 can (15 oz) kidney beans, drained and rinsed
- 1 can (15 oz) cannellini beans, drained and rinsed
- 1 cup small pasta (such as ditalini, small shells, or elbow macaroni)
- 1 teaspoon dried oregano
- 1 teaspoon dried basil
- Salt and pepper, to taste
- Fresh chopped parsley or basil, for garnish (optional)
- Grated Parmesan cheese, for serving (optional)

Instructions:

1. Sauté Vegetables: In a large pot or Dutch oven, heat olive oil over medium heat. Add chopped onion and sauté until translucent, about 5 minutes. Add minced garlic and sauté for another minute until fragrant.
2. Add Vegetables: Add diced carrots, celery, zucchini, yellow squash, and green beans to the pot. Sauté for about 5-7 minutes, until the vegetables begin to soften.
3. Add Tomatoes and Broth: Stir in diced tomatoes and cook for another 2-3 minutes. Pour in vegetable or chicken broth and bring the mixture to a boil.
4. Simmer: Reduce heat to low and let the soup simmer, uncovered, for about 15-20 minutes, or until the vegetables are tender.
5. Add Beans and Pasta: Add kidney beans, cannellini beans, and small pasta to the pot. Cook for an additional 10-12 minutes, or until the pasta is al dente and cooked through.
6. Season: Stir in dried oregano, dried basil, salt, and pepper to taste. Adjust seasoning as needed.
7. Serve: Ladle the minestrone soup into bowls. Garnish with fresh chopped parsley or basil, if desired. Serve hot, optionally topped with grated Parmesan cheese and crusty bread on the side.

Minestrone Soup is delicious and nutritious, packed with vegetables and beans. It's perfect for a satisfying meal on its own or as a starter. Feel free to customize the vegetables and herbs based on your preferences or what's in season. Enjoy your homemade minestrone soup!

Lentil Soup

Ingredients:

- 1 cup dried lentils (any variety you prefer)
- 2 tablespoons olive oil
- 1 onion, chopped
- 2 carrots, diced
- 2 celery stalks, diced
- 3 cloves garlic, minced
- 1 teaspoon ground cumin
- 1 teaspoon ground coriander
- 1/2 teaspoon smoked paprika (optional, for extra flavor)
- 6 cups vegetable or chicken broth
- 1 can (14 oz) diced tomatoes (or 1-2 fresh tomatoes, diced)
- 2 bay leaves
- Salt and pepper, to taste
- Fresh lemon juice, to taste (optional)
- Fresh parsley or cilantro, chopped, for garnish

Instructions:

1. Prepare Lentils: Rinse the dried lentils under cold water and drain.
2. Sauté Vegetables: In a large pot or Dutch oven, heat olive oil over medium heat. Add chopped onion, diced carrots, and diced celery. Sauté for about 5-7 minutes, until the vegetables start to soften.
3. Add Garlic and Spices: Add minced garlic, ground cumin, ground coriander, and smoked paprika (if using). Sauté for another 1-2 minutes until fragrant.
4. Add Broth and Tomatoes: Pour in vegetable or chicken broth and add diced tomatoes (with their juices). Stir well to combine.
5. Simmer: Add the drained lentils and bay leaves to the pot. Bring the soup to a boil, then reduce heat to low. Cover and let it simmer for about 20-25 minutes, or until the lentils are tender.
6. Season and Adjust Consistency: Remove the bay leaves from the soup. Season with salt and pepper to taste. If the soup is too thick for your liking, you can add more broth or water until you reach your desired consistency.
7. Finish and Serve: Stir in a squeeze of fresh lemon juice for a bright flavor (optional). Ladle the lentil soup into bowls. Garnish with chopped fresh parsley or cilantro. Serve hot, optionally with crusty bread or a side salad.

This lentil soup is nutritious, filling, and packed with flavor from the spices and vegetables. It's perfect for a comforting meal and can be easily customized with your favorite herbs or additional vegetables. Enjoy!

Potato Leek Soup

Ingredients:

- 3 leeks, white and light green parts only, sliced (about 3 cups)
- 3 tablespoons unsalted butter or olive oil
- 3 cloves garlic, minced
- 1 onion, chopped
- 3-4 large potatoes, peeled and diced (about 4 cups)
- 4 cups vegetable or chicken broth
- 1 bay leaf
- 1 teaspoon dried thyme
- Salt and pepper, to taste
- 1 cup heavy cream (optional, for extra creaminess)
- Fresh chives or parsley, chopped, for garnish

Instructions:

1. Prepare Leeks: Cut off the root ends of the leeks and slice them thinly. Rinse the sliced leeks thoroughly under cold water to remove any grit or dirt.
2. Sauté Vegetables: In a large pot or Dutch oven, melt butter over medium heat (or heat olive oil). Add sliced leeks, minced garlic, and chopped onion. Sauté for about 5-7 minutes, until the vegetables are softened and fragrant.
3. Add Potatoes and Broth: Add diced potatoes to the pot, along with vegetable or chicken broth, bay leaf, and dried thyme. Stir well to combine.
4. Simmer: Bring the mixture to a boil, then reduce heat to low. Cover and let it simmer for about 20-25 minutes, or until the potatoes are tender and can be easily pierced with a fork.
5. Blend Soup: Remove the bay leaf from the soup. Use an immersion blender directly in the pot to blend the soup until smooth and creamy. If you don't have an immersion blender, carefully transfer the soup in batches to a blender and blend until smooth, then return it to the pot.
6. Add Cream (optional) and Season: Stir in heavy cream, if using, to add extra creaminess to the soup. Season with salt and pepper to taste. Adjust seasoning as needed.
7. Serve: Ladle the potato leek soup into bowls. Garnish with chopped fresh chives or parsley. Serve hot, optionally with crusty bread or a side salad.

This potato leek soup is rich, creamy, and packed with flavor from the leeks and potatoes. It's perfect for a cozy meal and can be easily customized with additional herbs or spices to suit your taste. Enjoy!

Split Pea Soup

Ingredients:

- 1 pound (about 2 cups) dried split peas, rinsed and drained
- 2 tablespoons olive oil or butter
- 1 onion, chopped
- 2 carrots, diced
- 2 celery stalks, diced
- 3 cloves garlic, minced
- 8 cups vegetable or chicken broth
- 1 bay leaf
- 1 teaspoon dried thyme
- Salt and pepper, to taste
- 1-2 cups diced ham or smoked sausage (optional, for added flavor)
- Fresh parsley, chopped, for garnish (optional)

Instructions:

1. Sauté Vegetables: In a large pot or Dutch oven, heat olive oil or melt butter over medium heat. Add chopped onion, diced carrots, and diced celery. Sauté for about 5-7 minutes, until the vegetables start to soften.
2. Add Garlic and Split Peas: Add minced garlic and rinsed split peas to the pot. Stir well to combine with the vegetables.
3. Add Broth and Seasonings: Pour in vegetable or chicken broth. Add bay leaf and dried thyme. Stir to combine. Bring the mixture to a boil.
4. Simmer: Reduce heat to low and let the soup simmer, uncovered, for about 45-60 minutes, stirring occasionally. Cook until the split peas are tender and the soup has thickened to your desired consistency.
5. Optional: Add Meat (if using): If adding diced ham or smoked sausage for extra flavor, stir it into the soup during the last 15 minutes of cooking. This step is optional and can be omitted for a vegetarian version.
6. Season and Serve: Remove the bay leaf from the soup. Season with salt and pepper to taste. Adjust seasoning as needed.
7. Garnish and Serve: Ladle the split pea soup into bowls. Garnish with chopped fresh parsley, if desired. Serve hot, optionally with crusty bread or a side salad.

Split Pea Soup is deliciously thick and hearty, perfect for a comforting meal. It's great for leftovers and can be frozen for future meals. Enjoy the rich flavors of this classic soup!

Creamy Mushroom Soup

Ingredients:

- 1 pound (about 500g) mushrooms (cremini, button, or a mix), sliced
- 3 tablespoons unsalted butter
- 1 onion, finely chopped
- 2 cloves garlic, minced
- 1 teaspoon dried thyme (or 1 tablespoon fresh thyme leaves)
- Salt and pepper, to taste
- 1/4 cup all-purpose flour
- 4 cups vegetable or chicken broth
- 1 cup heavy cream
- 1/2 cup milk (optional, for lighter version)
- Fresh parsley, chopped, for garnish
- Croutons or toasted bread, for serving (optional)

Instructions:

1. Sauté Mushrooms: In a large pot or Dutch oven, melt butter over medium heat. Add sliced mushrooms and cook for about 5-7 minutes, stirring occasionally, until mushrooms are softened and browned. Remove a handful of mushrooms and set aside for garnish later, if desired.
2. Cook Aromatics: Add chopped onion and minced garlic to the pot with the mushrooms. Sauté for another 3-4 minutes until onion is translucent and garlic is fragrant. Stir in dried thyme, salt, and pepper.
3. Add Flour: Sprinkle flour over the mushroom mixture. Stir well to coat the mushrooms and cook for 1-2 minutes to remove the raw flour taste.
4. Add Broth and Simmer: Gradually pour in vegetable or chicken broth, stirring constantly to prevent lumps. Bring the mixture to a simmer and cook for about 10-15 minutes, stirring occasionally, until the soup has thickened slightly.
5. Blend Soup: Use an immersion blender directly in the pot to blend the soup until smooth. Alternatively, carefully transfer the soup in batches to a blender and blend until smooth, then return it to the pot.
6. Add Cream and Milk: Stir in heavy cream and milk (if using) to the soup. Heat gently over low heat, stirring occasionally, until heated through. Do not boil once the cream has been added.
7. Adjust Seasoning and Serve: Taste and adjust seasoning with salt and pepper as needed. If the soup is too thick, you can add a bit more broth or milk to reach your desired consistency.
8. Serve: Ladle the creamy mushroom soup into bowls. Garnish with reserved sautéed mushrooms, chopped fresh parsley, and optionally serve with croutons or toasted bread on the side.

Creamy Mushroom Soup is perfect for a cozy meal, especially on colder days. The combination of mushrooms, thyme, and creamy texture makes it a comforting dish that's sure to please. Enjoy!

Thai Coconut Soup (Tom Kha Gai)

Ingredients:

- 1 tablespoon vegetable oil
- 2-3 tablespoons Thai red curry paste (adjust to taste)
- 3-4 cups chicken broth or vegetable broth
- 1 can (14 oz) coconut milk
- 1 stalk lemongrass, bruised and cut into 2-inch pieces
- 3-4 slices galangal or ginger
- 1-2 Thai bird's eye chilies, sliced (adjust to spice preference)
- 1 medium onion, thinly sliced
- 1 red bell pepper, thinly sliced
- 1 cup mushrooms, sliced (such as straw mushrooms or cremini)
- 1 pound boneless, skinless chicken thighs or breasts, thinly sliced
- 2 tablespoons fish sauce (or soy sauce for vegetarian)
- 1-2 tablespoons palm sugar or brown sugar (adjust to taste)
- 1-2 tablespoons lime juice (adjust to taste)
- Fresh cilantro leaves, for garnish
- Thai basil leaves, for garnish (optional)
- Sliced red chili peppers, for garnish (optional)

Instructions:

1. Prepare Aromatics: In a large pot or Dutch oven, heat vegetable oil over medium heat. Add Thai red curry paste and cook for about 1-2 minutes until fragrant.
2. Add Broth and Coconut Milk: Pour in chicken broth and coconut milk. Stir well to combine and bring to a gentle simmer over medium heat.
3. Infuse Flavors: Add lemongrass pieces, galangal or ginger slices, sliced Thai bird's eye chilies, and thinly sliced onion to the pot. Let them simmer together for about 5 minutes to infuse the flavors into the broth.
4. Add Vegetables and Chicken: Add thinly sliced red bell pepper, sliced mushrooms, and thinly sliced chicken to the pot. Cook for about 5-7 minutes, or until the chicken is cooked through and vegetables are tender.
5. Season the Soup: Stir in fish sauce (or soy sauce for vegetarian option), palm sugar (or brown sugar), and lime juice. Taste and adjust the seasoning by adding more fish sauce for saltiness, sugar for sweetness, or lime juice for sourness, according to your preference.
6. Serve: Remove lemongrass stalks and galangal or ginger slices from the soup. Ladle the Thai Coconut Soup into bowls. Garnish with fresh cilantro leaves, Thai basil leaves (if using), and sliced red chili peppers for extra heat if desired.
7. Enjoy: Serve hot and enjoy this fragrant and flavorful Thai Coconut Soup on its own or with steamed jasmine rice for a complete meal.

This Tom Kha Gai recipe brings together the wonderful flavors of Thai cuisine, creating a soup that's creamy, spicy, and utterly delicious. Adjust the spice level and sweetness to your liking for a personalized experience.

Gazpacho

Ingredients:

- 6 ripe tomatoes, chopped
- 1 cucumber, peeled, seeded, and chopped
- 1 red bell pepper, seeded and chopped
- 1 green bell pepper, seeded and chopped
- 1 small red onion, chopped
- 2 cloves garlic, minced
- 3 cups tomato juice or vegetable juice (like V8)
- 1/4 cup extra-virgin olive oil
- 2 tablespoons red wine vinegar or sherry vinegar
- 1 teaspoon salt, or to taste
- 1/2 teaspoon ground black pepper
- 1/2 teaspoon ground cumin (optional)
- 1/4 teaspoon cayenne pepper (optional, for spice)
- 1/2 cup fresh basil leaves, chopped
- Croutons, diced cucumber, or diced bell pepper for garnish (optional)

Instructions:

1. Prepare Vegetables: In a large bowl, combine chopped tomatoes, cucumber, red bell pepper, green bell pepper, red onion, and minced garlic.
2. Blend Soup: Working in batches if needed, transfer the vegetable mixture to a blender or food processor. Add tomato juice, olive oil, red wine vinegar, salt, black pepper, ground cumin (if using), and cayenne pepper (if using). Blend until smooth.
3. Adjust Consistency: If the gazpacho is too thick, add more tomato juice or water to reach your desired consistency. Taste and adjust seasoning as needed, adding more salt, vinegar, or spices to taste.
4. Chill: Cover the gazpacho and refrigerate for at least 2 hours, or until well chilled. Chilling allows the flavors to meld together.
5. Serve: Stir the gazpacho well before serving. Ladle into bowls and garnish with chopped fresh basil leaves. Optionally, garnish with croutons, diced cucumber, or diced bell pepper for added texture and freshness.
6. Enjoy: Serve chilled and enjoy this refreshing Gazpacho as a light appetizer or a cool soup on a hot day.

Gazpacho is best served cold and can be stored in the refrigerator for a few days. It's a versatile recipe, so feel free to adjust the ingredients and seasonings based on your preferences. It's a wonderful way to enjoy the bounty of summer vegetables in a delicious and healthy soup.

Beef Stew Soup

Ingredients:

- 1.5 pounds stew beef, cut into bite-sized pieces
- 2 tablespoons olive oil
- 1 onion, chopped
- 3 cloves garlic, minced
- 4 carrots, peeled and sliced
- 3 celery stalks, sliced
- 2 potatoes, peeled and diced
- 1 can (14 oz) diced tomatoes
- 4 cups beef broth
- 1 cup red wine (optional)
- 2 bay leaves
- 1 teaspoon dried thyme
- Salt and pepper, to taste
- 2 tablespoons Worcestershire sauce
- 2 tablespoons tomato paste
- Chopped fresh parsley, for garnish (optional)

Instructions:

1. Brown the Beef: In a large pot or Dutch oven, heat olive oil over medium-high heat. Add the stew beef pieces and brown them on all sides. You may need to do this in batches to avoid overcrowding the pot. Remove the browned beef and set aside.
2. Sauté Vegetables: In the same pot, add chopped onion and garlic. Sauté for 2-3 minutes until onions are translucent and garlic is fragrant.
3. Combine Ingredients: Add sliced carrots, sliced celery, diced potatoes, diced tomatoes (with their juices), beef broth, and red wine (if using) to the pot. Stir well to combine.
4. Add Seasonings: Add bay leaves, dried thyme, salt, pepper, Worcestershire sauce, and tomato paste to the pot. Stir again to incorporate all ingredients.
5. Simmer: Bring the mixture to a boil, then reduce heat to low. Cover and let the soup simmer for about 1.5 to 2 hours, stirring occasionally, until the beef is tender and the vegetables are cooked through.
6. Adjust Consistency and Seasoning: If the soup is too thick, add more beef broth or water to reach your desired consistency. Taste and adjust seasoning with salt and pepper as needed.
7. Serve: Remove the bay leaves from the soup. Ladle the beef stew soup into bowls. Garnish with chopped fresh parsley if desired. Serve hot and enjoy!

This beef stew soup is rich in flavor and perfect for a comforting meal. It pairs well with crusty bread or biscuits for dipping into the broth. It's also a great dish to make ahead as the flavors develop even more overnight. Enjoy this hearty and satisfying beef stew soup!

Clam Chowder

Ingredients:

- 4 slices bacon, diced (optional)
- 1 onion, chopped
- 2 celery stalks, diced
- 3 tablespoons unsalted butter
- 3 tablespoons all-purpose flour
- 3 cups chicken broth or seafood broth
- 1 cup heavy cream
- 2 cups potatoes, peeled and diced
- 2 cans (6.5 oz each) chopped clams, drained, juice reserved
- 1 bay leaf
- Salt and pepper, to taste
- Fresh parsley, chopped, for garnish (optional)
- Oyster crackers or crusty bread, for serving

Instructions:

1. Cook Bacon (if using): In a large pot or Dutch oven, cook diced bacon over medium heat until crispy. Remove bacon with a slotted spoon and set aside on a paper towel-lined plate. Leave about 1 tablespoon of bacon fat in the pot.
2. Sauté Vegetables: Add chopped onion and diced celery to the pot. Sauté for about 5 minutes, until onions are translucent and celery is softened.
3. Make Roux: Add butter to the pot and let it melt. Stir in flour to create a roux, stirring constantly for about 1-2 minutes until the mixture becomes lightly golden brown.
4. Add Broth and Potatoes: Gradually pour in chicken broth or seafood broth, stirring constantly to avoid lumps. Add diced potatoes and reserved clam juice (from the cans). Stir well to combine.
5. Simmer Chowder: Add the bay leaf and bring the mixture to a simmer. Let it cook for about 10-15 minutes, or until the potatoes are tender and cooked through.
6. Add Clams and Cream: Stir in chopped clams (from the cans) and heavy cream. Let the chowder simmer for another 5-10 minutes to heat through. Be careful not to let the chowder boil once the cream has been added.
7. Season and Serve: Season with salt and pepper to taste. Remove the bay leaf from the chowder. Ladle the clam chowder into bowls. Garnish with crispy bacon (if using) and chopped fresh parsley. Serve hot, accompanied by oyster crackers or crusty bread for dipping.

Clam chowder is best enjoyed fresh and hot, straight from the stove. It's a comforting and flavorful soup that's perfect for a cozy meal, especially during colder months. Adjust the thickness of the chowder by adding more broth or cream as desired. Enjoy!

Corn Chowder

Ingredients:

- 4 slices bacon, chopped (optional)
- 1 onion, chopped
- 2 celery stalks, diced
- 2 carrots, diced
- 3 tablespoons unsalted butter
- 3 tablespoons all-purpose flour
- 4 cups chicken or vegetable broth
- 4 cups fresh or frozen corn kernels (about 6-8 ears of corn)
- 2 medium potatoes, peeled and diced
- 1 bay leaf
- 1 teaspoon dried thyme (or use fresh thyme leaves)
- 1 cup heavy cream
- Salt and pepper, to taste
- Fresh parsley or chives, chopped, for garnish (optional)

Instructions:

1. Cook Bacon (if using): In a large pot or Dutch oven, cook chopped bacon over medium heat until crispy. Remove bacon with a slotted spoon and set aside on a paper towel-lined plate. Leave about 1 tablespoon of bacon fat in the pot.
2. Sauté Vegetables: Add chopped onion, diced celery, and diced carrots to the pot. Sauté for about 5 minutes, until onions are translucent and vegetables are softened.
3. Make Roux: Add butter to the pot and let it melt. Stir in flour to create a roux, stirring constantly for about 1-2 minutes until the mixture becomes lightly golden brown.
4. Add Broth and Potatoes: Gradually pour in chicken or vegetable broth, stirring constantly to avoid lumps. Add diced potatoes, corn kernels, bay leaf, and dried thyme. Stir well to combine.
5. Simmer Chowder: Bring the mixture to a simmer. Let it cook for about 15-20 minutes, or until the potatoes are tender and cooked through.
6. Blend Soup (optional): For a creamier texture, you can blend a portion of the soup using an immersion blender or by transferring a portion to a blender and blending until smooth. This step is optional depending on your preference.
7. Add Cream and Seasoning: Stir in heavy cream and let the chowder simmer for another 5-10 minutes to heat through. Season with salt and pepper to taste.
8. Serve: Ladle the corn chowder into bowls. Garnish with crispy bacon (if using), chopped fresh parsley or chives, and a sprinkle of black pepper. Serve hot, optionally with crusty bread or oyster crackers on the side.

Corn chowder is a comforting and versatile soup that's perfect for using fresh summer corn or frozen corn year-round. It's creamy, hearty, and full of flavor, making it a favorite for both lunch and dinner. Enjoy this delicious homemade corn chowder!

Borscht (Beet Soup)

Ingredients:

- 2 tablespoons olive oil or vegetable oil
- 1 onion, finely chopped
- 2-3 cloves garlic, minced
- 3 medium beets, peeled and grated
- 2 carrots, peeled and grated
- 2 potatoes, peeled and diced
- 4 cups vegetable or beef broth
- 1 can (14 oz) diced tomatoes
- 1 tablespoon tomato paste
- 1 bay leaf
- 1 teaspoon dried dill (or 1 tablespoon fresh dill, chopped)
- Salt and pepper, to taste
- 1 tablespoon red wine vinegar or lemon juice
- Sour cream, for serving
- Fresh dill, chopped, for garnish (optional)

Instructions:

1. Sauté Vegetables: Heat olive oil in a large pot or Dutch oven over medium heat. Add chopped onion and minced garlic. Sauté for about 5 minutes, until onions are translucent and garlic is fragrant.
2. Add Beets and Carrots: Add grated beets and grated carrots to the pot. Cook, stirring occasionally, for about 10 minutes, until vegetables are softened.
3. Add Potatoes and Broth: Add diced potatoes, vegetable or beef broth, diced tomatoes (with their juices), tomato paste, bay leaf, and dried dill (if using dried). Stir well to combine.
4. Simmer: Bring the mixture to a boil, then reduce heat to low. Cover and let the soup simmer for about 30-40 minutes, or until all vegetables are tender.
5. Season and Finish: Season the borscht with salt and pepper to taste. Stir in red wine vinegar or lemon juice for a slight tangy flavor adjustment.
6. Serve: Ladle the borscht into bowls. Serve hot, garnished with a dollop of sour cream and chopped fresh dill, if desired. Accompany with crusty bread or garlic bread.

Borscht can be enjoyed hot or cold, depending on personal preference. It's nutritious, flavorful, and provides a wonderful balance of sweet and savory flavors from the beets and other vegetables. This recipe offers a classic rendition of this beloved Eastern European soup.

Tortilla Soup

Ingredients:

- 2 tablespoons vegetable oil
- 1 onion, chopped
- 3 cloves garlic, minced
- 1 jalapeño, seeded and finely chopped (optional, for heat)
- 1 red bell pepper, chopped
- 1 green bell pepper, chopped
- 1 can (14 oz) diced tomatoes
- 1 teaspoon ground cumin
- 1 teaspoon chili powder
- 1/2 teaspoon smoked paprika (optional, for smoky flavor)
- 6 cups chicken or vegetable broth
- 1 cup corn kernels (fresh or frozen)
- 1 can (15 oz) black beans, drained and rinsed
- Salt and pepper, to taste
- Juice of 1 lime
- Fresh cilantro, chopped, for garnish
- Avocado slices, for garnish
- Tortilla chips or strips, for garnish
- Shredded cheese (such as Monterey Jack or cheddar), for garnish (optional)
- Sour cream or Mexican crema, for garnish (optional)

Instructions:

1. Sauté Aromatics: In a large pot or Dutch oven, heat vegetable oil over medium heat. Add chopped onion, minced garlic, and jalapeño (if using). Sauté for about 3-4 minutes, until onions are translucent and fragrant.
2. Add Peppers and Spices: Add chopped red bell pepper and green bell pepper to the pot. Sauté for another 3-4 minutes until peppers begin to soften. Stir in ground cumin, chili powder, and smoked paprika (if using), cooking for 1 minute until fragrant.
3. Simmer Soup: Pour in diced tomatoes (with their juices) and chicken or vegetable broth. Bring the mixture to a boil, then reduce heat to low. Cover and let it simmer for about 15-20 minutes, allowing the flavors to meld together.
4. Add Corn and Beans: Stir in corn kernels and black beans. Simmer for another 5 minutes to heat through. Season with salt and pepper to taste.
5. Finish and Serve: Remove the soup from heat. Stir in fresh lime juice for a burst of citrus flavor.
6. Prepare Tortilla Strips: While the soup is simmering, prepare tortilla strips or chips by slicing corn tortillas into thin strips or triangles. Heat a small amount of vegetable oil in a skillet over medium-high heat. Fry the tortilla strips until golden and crispy, then drain on paper towels.

7. Serve: Ladle the tortilla soup into bowls. Top each serving with a handful of tortilla strips, chopped fresh cilantro, avocado slices, shredded cheese (if using), and a dollop of sour cream or Mexican crema (if desired).

Tortilla soup is versatile and can be customized with your favorite toppings. It's a delicious and satisfying meal that's perfect for any time of year. Enjoy this flavorful Mexican-inspired soup!

Ramen Soup

Ingredients:

For the Broth:

- 6 cups chicken broth (homemade or store-bought)
- 2 cups water
- 2 cloves garlic, minced
- 1-inch piece of ginger, peeled and sliced
- 2 tablespoons soy sauce
- 1 tablespoon mirin (Japanese sweet rice wine) or rice vinegar
- 1 tablespoon sesame oil
- 1 tablespoon miso paste (optional, for extra depth of flavor)

For the Toppings and Noodles:

- 4 packs of instant ramen noodles (discard seasoning packets)
- 4 soft-boiled eggs, peeled and halved
- 2 cups baby spinach or bok choy leaves
- 1 cup sliced shiitake mushrooms (or any mushrooms of your choice)
- 1 cup sliced green onions (scallions)
- 1 sheet nori (seaweed), cut into strips (optional)
- Toasted sesame seeds, for garnish (optional)
- Red pepper flakes or shichimi togarashi (Japanese seven spice blend), for extra spice (optional)

Instructions:

1. Prepare Broth: In a large pot, combine chicken broth, water, minced garlic, sliced ginger, soy sauce, mirin or rice vinegar, sesame oil, and miso paste (if using). Bring to a boil over medium-high heat, then reduce heat to low and let it simmer for about 15-20 minutes to allow the flavors to meld together. Remove and discard the ginger slices before serving.
2. Prepare Toppings: While the broth is simmering, prepare the toppings. Soft-boil the eggs (about 6-7 minutes in boiling water), then peel and halve them. Prepare the baby spinach or bok choy leaves, sliced mushrooms, and green onions. Set aside.
3. Cook Ramen Noodles: Cook the instant ramen noodles according to the package instructions, usually about 2-3 minutes in boiling water. Drain and rinse under cold water to stop the cooking process. Divide the noodles among serving bowls.
4. Assemble Ramen Soup: Ladle the hot broth over the cooked noodles in each bowl. Arrange the soft-boiled eggs, baby spinach or bok choy leaves, sliced mushrooms, and green onions on top of the noodles.
5. Garnish and Serve: Garnish the ramen soup with nori strips, toasted sesame seeds, and red pepper flakes or shichimi togarashi for extra spice if desired.

6. Enjoy: Serve hot and enjoy your homemade ramen soup immediately. Mix the toppings into the broth and noodles before eating for the best flavor experience.

This homemade ramen soup is versatile, and you can customize it with your favorite toppings such as sliced bamboo shoots, corn kernels, or sliced pork or chicken. It's a comforting and satisfying meal that's perfect for any time of year.

Chicken Tortilla Soup

Ingredients:

- 1 tablespoon vegetable oil
- 1 onion, diced
- 3 cloves garlic, minced
- 1 jalapeño, seeded and finely chopped (optional, for heat)
- 1 red bell pepper, diced
- 1 green bell pepper, diced
- 1 teaspoon ground cumin
- 1 teaspoon chili powder
- 1/2 teaspoon smoked paprika (optional)
- 6 cups chicken broth
- 1 can (14 oz) diced tomatoes
- 1 can (4 oz) diced green chilies
- 2 cups shredded cooked chicken (rotisserie chicken works well)
- Salt and pepper, to taste
- Juice of 1 lime
- 1 cup frozen corn kernels
- 1/4 cup chopped fresh cilantro
- Tortilla chips, for serving
- Avocado slices, for serving
- Shredded cheese (such as Monterey Jack or cheddar), for serving (optional)
- Sour cream or Mexican crema, for serving (optional)

Instructions:

1. Sauté Aromatics: Heat vegetable oil in a large pot or Dutch oven over medium heat. Add diced onion, minced garlic, and jalapeño (if using). Sauté for about 3-4 minutes until onions are translucent and fragrant.
2. Add Peppers and Spices: Add diced red bell pepper and green bell pepper to the pot. Sauté for another 3-4 minutes until peppers begin to soften. Stir in ground cumin, chili powder, and smoked paprika (if using), cooking for 1 minute until fragrant.
3. Simmer Soup: Pour in chicken broth, diced tomatoes (with their juices), and diced green chilies. Bring the mixture to a boil, then reduce heat to low. Let it simmer for about 15-20 minutes to allow flavors to meld together.
4. Add Chicken and Corn: Stir in shredded cooked chicken, frozen corn kernels, and continue to simmer for another 5-10 minutes until chicken is heated through and corn is tender.
5. Season and Finish: Season the soup with salt, pepper, and lime juice to taste. Stir in chopped fresh cilantro.
6. Serve: Ladle the chicken tortilla soup into bowls. Serve hot, garnished with tortilla chips for crunch, avocado slices, shredded cheese (if using), and a dollop of sour cream or Mexican crema if desired.

7. Enjoy: Enjoy this flavorful and hearty chicken tortilla soup immediately. It's perfect for a cozy meal and can be easily customized with your favorite toppings.

This soup is not only delicious but also a great way to use leftover chicken. The combination of spices, vegetables, and toppings makes it a satisfying and comforting dish that's sure to be a hit at the dinner table.

Italian Wedding Soup

Ingredients:

For the Meatballs:

- 1/2 pound ground beef
- 1/2 pound ground pork
- 1/4 cup breadcrumbs
- 1/4 cup grated Parmesan cheese
- 1/4 cup fresh parsley, chopped
- 1 egg, beaten
- 2 cloves garlic, minced
- Salt and pepper, to taste

For the Soup:

- 1 tablespoon olive oil
- 1 onion, chopped
- 2 carrots, peeled and diced
- 2 celery stalks, diced
- 3 cloves garlic, minced
- 8 cups chicken broth
- 1 cup small pasta (such as acini di pepe or orzo)
- 4 cups fresh spinach or escarole, chopped
- 1/4 cup grated Parmesan cheese, for serving
- Fresh parsley, chopped, for garnish (optional)
- Salt and pepper, to taste

Instructions:

1. Prepare the Meatballs:
    - In a large bowl, combine ground beef, ground pork, breadcrumbs, grated Parmesan, chopped parsley, beaten egg, minced garlic, salt, and pepper. Mix well until all ingredients are evenly incorporated.
    - Roll the mixture into small meatballs, about 1 inch in diameter. Place them on a baking sheet or plate.
2. Brown the Meatballs:
    - In a large pot or Dutch oven, heat olive oil over medium heat. Add the meatballs in batches and cook until they are browned on all sides. Remove the browned meatballs and set them aside.
3. Sauté the Vegetables:
    - In the same pot, add chopped onion, diced carrots, and diced celery. Sauté for about 5 minutes until the vegetables are softened. Add minced garlic and cook for another 1-2 minutes until fragrant.

4. Simmer the Soup:
    - Pour in the chicken broth and bring it to a boil. Add the browned meatballs back into the pot. Reduce the heat to low and let the soup simmer for about 20-25 minutes, until the meatballs are cooked through and the vegetables are tender.
5. Cook the Pasta:
    - In a separate pot, cook the small pasta according to the package instructions until al dente. Drain and set aside.
6. Add Greens and Pasta:
    - Stir in the chopped spinach or escarole and the cooked pasta into the soup. Let it simmer for another 5 minutes until the greens are wilted and tender.
7. Season and Serve:
    - Taste the soup and season with salt and pepper as needed. Ladle the soup into bowls and sprinkle with grated Parmesan cheese and chopped fresh parsley, if desired.
8. Enjoy:
    - Serve hot with crusty bread on the side for a comforting and hearty meal.

Italian Wedding Soup is a delightful combination of flavors and textures, perfect for a satisfying lunch or dinner. The tender meatballs, flavorful broth, and fresh greens make it a family favorite. Enjoy!

Avgolemono (Greek Lemon Chicken Soup)

Ingredients:

- 6 cups chicken broth
- 1 cup cooked chicken, shredded or diced
- 1/2 cup uncooked rice or orzo pasta
- 3 large eggs
- 1/3 cup fresh lemon juice (about 2-3 lemons)
- Salt and pepper, to taste
- Fresh dill or parsley, chopped, for garnish (optional)

Instructions:

1. Cook the Rice/Orzo:
    - In a large pot, bring the chicken broth to a boil. Add the rice or orzo and cook until tender, about 15-20 minutes. Reduce heat to low and keep the broth at a gentle simmer.
2. Prepare the Egg-Lemon Mixture:
    - In a medium bowl, whisk together the eggs and fresh lemon juice until well combined and slightly frothy.
3. Temper the Eggs:
    - Slowly ladle about 1 cup of hot broth from the pot into the egg-lemon mixture, whisking constantly to prevent the eggs from curdling. This step is crucial as it gradually warms the eggs.
4. Combine and Thicken:
    - Slowly pour the tempered egg-lemon mixture back into the pot with the remaining broth, whisking constantly. Continue to cook over low heat, stirring gently, until the soup thickens slightly. Do not let it boil, as this can cause the eggs to curdle.
5. Add Chicken and Season:
    - Stir in the shredded or diced chicken. Season with salt and pepper to taste. Allow the soup to heat through for a few more minutes, stirring occasionally.
6. Serve:
    - Ladle the avgolemono into bowls. Garnish with freshly chopped dill or parsley, if desired.
7. Enjoy:
    - Serve hot, accompanied by crusty bread for a complete meal.

Avgolemono soup is a wonderfully comforting and flavorful dish, perfect for any time of the year. The combination of lemon and chicken creates a refreshing yet hearty soup that's sure to become a favorite. Enjoy!

Miso Soup

Ingredients:

- 4 cups dashi broth (homemade or store-bought)
- 3-4 tablespoons miso paste (white or yellow miso)
- 1/2 cup firm tofu, cut into small cubes
- 1/4 cup wakame seaweed, rehydrated (if using dried)
- 2 green onions, thinly sliced

Instructions:

1. Prepare Dashi Broth:
     - If making dashi from scratch, prepare it according to your recipe. Otherwise, bring the store-bought dashi broth to a gentle simmer in a medium pot.
2. Rehydrate Seaweed:
     - If using dried wakame seaweed, rehydrate it by soaking it in water for about 5 minutes. Once it's rehydrated, drain and set aside.
3. Add Tofu:
     - Add the cubed tofu to the simmering dashi broth. Let it cook for about 2-3 minutes.
4. Incorporate Miso Paste:
     - Place the miso paste in a small bowl. Ladle a small amount of the hot dashi broth into the bowl with the miso paste and whisk until the miso is completely dissolved and smooth.
     - Slowly pour the dissolved miso mixture back into the pot, stirring gently to combine. Be careful not to let the soup boil once the miso is added, as it can affect the flavor and texture.
5. Add Seaweed:
     - Stir in the rehydrated wakame seaweed. Let the soup heat through for another minute or so.
6. Serve:
     - Ladle the miso soup into bowls. Garnish with thinly sliced green onions.
7. Enjoy:
     - Serve hot as a starter or alongside a main dish in a Japanese meal.

Miso soup is a simple yet deeply flavorful dish, perfect as a comforting starter or a light meal. The combination of miso paste, tofu, seaweed, and green onions creates a balanced and nutritious soup that's both soothing and satisfying. Enjoy your homemade miso soup!

Pho (Vietnamese Noodle Soup)

Ingredients:

For the Broth:

- 2 large onions, halved
- 4-inch piece of ginger, sliced
- 5-6 pounds beef bones (marrow and knuckle bones)
- 1 pound beef brisket or chuck
- 5 star anise
- 6 whole cloves
- 1 cinnamon stick
- 1 tablespoon coriander seeds
- 1 tablespoon fennel seeds
- 1 tablespoon salt
- 1/4 cup fish sauce
- 2 tablespoons rock sugar or regular sugar
- 8-10 cups water

For the Soup:

- 1 pound rice noodles (banh pho)
- 1/2 pound beef sirloin or eye of round, thinly sliced
- Fresh herbs (cilantro, Thai basil, mint)
- Bean sprouts
- Lime wedges
- Thinly sliced red or green chili peppers
- Hoisin sauce and Sriracha, for serving
- Thinly sliced onions and green onions, for garnish

Instructions:

1. Char the Aromatics:
    - Preheat your broiler. Place the halved onions and sliced ginger on a baking sheet. Broil for about 5-10 minutes until they are charred, flipping halfway through.
2. Prepare the Broth:
    - In a large pot, add the beef bones and cover with water. Bring to a boil and let it boil for 5 minutes. Drain and rinse the bones to remove impurities.
    - In the same pot, add the cleaned bones, charred onions, and ginger. Add beef brisket or chuck. Cover with 8-10 cups of water and bring to a boil. Reduce heat and simmer.
3. Toast the Spices:

- In a dry skillet, toast the star anise, cloves, cinnamon stick, coriander seeds, and fennel seeds over medium heat until fragrant (about 2-3 minutes). Add the toasted spices to the pot.
4. Simmer the Broth:
    - Add salt, fish sauce, and rock sugar to the pot. Simmer for at least 3-4 hours, skimming any impurities that rise to the surface. For a richer broth, simmer for up to 6-8 hours. Remove the brisket after 1.5-2 hours or until tender. Set it aside to cool, then slice thinly.
5. Strain the Broth:
    - Once the broth is done, strain it through a fine mesh sieve into a clean pot. Discard the solids and keep the broth hot over low heat.
6. Prepare the Noodles:
    - Cook the rice noodles according to package instructions. Drain and set aside.
7. Assemble the Pho:
    - Divide the cooked noodles among serving bowls. Top with thin slices of raw beef sirloin or eye of round and the cooked, sliced brisket.
    - Ladle the hot broth over the noodles and beef, cooking the raw beef slices in the broth.
8. Garnish and Serve:
    - Serve the pho with fresh herbs, bean sprouts, lime wedges, sliced chili peppers, and thinly sliced onions and green onions. Offer hoisin sauce and Sriracha on the side for additional flavor.

Enjoy this authentic and aromatic Vietnamese pho, perfect for a satisfying meal that's rich in flavor and tradition!

Moroccan Harira Soup

Ingredients:

- 2 tablespoons olive oil
- 1 onion, finely chopped
- 2 celery stalks, finely chopped
- 2 carrots, peeled and diced
- 3 cloves garlic, minced
- 1 teaspoon ground turmeric
- 1 teaspoon ground cinnamon
- 1 teaspoon ground ginger
- 1 teaspoon ground cumin
- 1/2 teaspoon ground black pepper
- 1/4 teaspoon ground cayenne pepper (optional)
- 1 cup green or brown lentils, rinsed
- 1 can (15 oz) chickpeas, drained and rinsed
- 1 can (15 oz) diced tomatoes
- 6 cups vegetable or chicken broth
- 1/4 cup fresh cilantro, chopped
- 1/4 cup fresh parsley, chopped
- 1/2 cup broken vermicelli or small pasta
- Juice of 1 lemon
- Salt, to taste

Instructions:

1. Sauté Aromatics:
   - In a large pot or Dutch oven, heat the olive oil over medium heat. Add the finely chopped onion, celery, and carrots. Sauté for about 5 minutes until the vegetables are softened.
   - Add minced garlic and cook for another 1-2 minutes until fragrant.
2. Add Spices:
   - Stir in ground turmeric, cinnamon, ginger, cumin, black pepper, and cayenne pepper (if using). Cook for 1-2 minutes, stirring constantly, until the spices are fragrant.
3. Simmer the Soup:
   - Add the rinsed lentils, chickpeas, diced tomatoes (with their juices), and vegetable or chicken broth to the pot. Stir to combine.
   - Bring the mixture to a boil, then reduce the heat to low. Cover and let the soup simmer for about 30-40 minutes until the lentils are tender.
4. Add Fresh Herbs and Pasta:
   - Stir in the chopped fresh cilantro and parsley. Add the broken vermicelli or small pasta. Continue to simmer for another 10-15 minutes until the pasta is cooked.
5. Finish and Season:

        - Stir in the juice of 1 lemon. Taste the soup and adjust the seasoning with salt as needed.
6. Serve:
        - Ladle the Harira into bowls. Garnish with additional fresh cilantro and parsley if desired.
7. Enjoy:
        - Serve hot with a side of crusty bread or flatbread. Harira can also be accompanied by dates or a wedge of lemon.

This Moroccan Harira is a nourishing and flavorful soup, perfect for any time of the year but especially comforting during cooler months. The combination of spices, herbs, and hearty ingredients makes it a satisfying and aromatic dish. Enjoy your homemade Harira!

Pumpkin Soup

Ingredients:

- 2 tablespoons olive oil or butter
- 1 onion, chopped
- 3 cloves garlic, minced
- 1 teaspoon ground ginger
- 1/2 teaspoon ground cumin
- 1/4 teaspoon ground nutmeg
- 1/4 teaspoon ground cinnamon
- 4 cups pumpkin puree (canned or homemade)
- 4 cups vegetable or chicken broth
- 1 cup heavy cream or coconut milk
- Salt and pepper, to taste
- Fresh parsley or chives, chopped, for garnish
- Pumpkin seeds, for garnish (optional)

Instructions:

1. Sauté Aromatics:
    - In a large pot, heat the olive oil or butter over medium heat. Add the chopped onion and sauté for about 5 minutes until it is soft and translucent.
    - Add the minced garlic and cook for another 1-2 minutes until fragrant.
2. Add Spices:
    - Stir in the ground ginger, cumin, nutmeg, and cinnamon. Cook for 1 minute, stirring constantly, until the spices are fragrant.
3. Add Pumpkin and Broth:
    - Add the pumpkin puree and vegetable or chicken broth to the pot. Stir well to combine.
    - Bring the mixture to a boil, then reduce the heat to low. Let it simmer for about 15-20 minutes to allow the flavors to meld together.
4. Blend the Soup:
    - Use an immersion blender to puree the soup until smooth. Alternatively, you can transfer the soup in batches to a countertop blender and blend until smooth, then return it to the pot.
5. Add Cream and Season:
    - Stir in the heavy cream or coconut milk. Heat the soup gently over low heat until warmed through. Do not let it boil.
    - Season with salt and pepper to taste.
6. Serve:
    - Ladle the pumpkin soup into bowls. Garnish with chopped fresh parsley or chives and a sprinkle of pumpkin seeds if desired.
7. Enjoy:

- - Serve hot with a side of crusty bread or a dollop of sour cream or yogurt if you like.

This creamy pumpkin soup is rich, flavorful, and perfect for a cozy meal. The blend of spices adds warmth and depth, making it a delightful dish to enjoy during the cooler months.

Wonton Soup

Ingredients:

For the Wontons:

- 1/2 pound ground pork
- 1/4 pound shrimp, peeled, deveined, and finely chopped
- 2 green onions, finely chopped
- 1 tablespoon soy sauce
- 1 tablespoon sesame oil
- 1 tablespoon rice wine or dry sherry
- 1 teaspoon grated fresh ginger
- 1 teaspoon cornstarch
- 1/4 teaspoon white pepper
- 30-40 wonton wrappers

For the Broth:

- 6 cups chicken broth
- 1-inch piece of ginger, sliced
- 2 cloves garlic, smashed
- 2 tablespoons soy sauce
- 1 tablespoon rice wine or dry sherry
- 1 teaspoon sesame oil
- Salt and pepper, to taste
- 2-3 green onions, sliced for garnish
- Fresh cilantro, chopped for garnish (optional)
- Baby bok choy or spinach, for garnish (optional)

Instructions:

1. Prepare the Wontons:
    - In a large bowl, combine the ground pork, chopped shrimp, finely chopped green onions, soy sauce, sesame oil, rice wine or sherry, grated ginger, cornstarch, and white pepper. Mix well until the ingredients are evenly combined.
    - Place a wonton wrapper on a clean surface. Add about 1 teaspoon of the filling in the center of the wrapper.
    - Moisten the edges of the wrapper with water. Fold the wrapper in half to form a triangle, sealing the edges tightly to encase the filling. Bring the two bottom corners of the triangle together, moisten one of the corners with water, and press them together to seal. Repeat with the remaining wonton wrappers and filling.
2. Prepare the Broth:

- In a large pot, bring the chicken broth to a boil. Add the sliced ginger and smashed garlic cloves. Reduce heat and let it simmer for about 10 minutes to infuse the flavors.
- Add soy sauce, rice wine or sherry, and sesame oil to the broth. Season with salt and pepper to taste.
3. Cook the Wontons:
    - Bring the broth to a gentle boil. Carefully add the wontons to the pot, a few at a time, to avoid overcrowding. Cook for about 4-5 minutes, or until the wontons float to the surface and are cooked through.
    - If using, add the baby bok choy or spinach to the pot during the last minute of cooking to wilt.
4. Serve:
    - Remove the ginger and garlic slices from the broth. Ladle the wonton soup into bowls, making sure to include several wontons in each serving.
    - Garnish with sliced green onions and chopped fresh cilantro, if desired.
5. Enjoy:
    - Serve hot and enjoy your comforting bowl of homemade wonton soup.

This classic wonton soup is a perfect balance of savory flavors and tender textures, making it a delightful dish for any occasion. Enjoy!

Cream of Broccoli Soup

Ingredients:

- 2 tablespoons butter
- 1 onion, chopped
- 2 cloves garlic, minced
- 4 cups fresh broccoli florets
- 1 large potato, peeled and diced
- 4 cups vegetable or chicken broth
- 1 cup heavy cream
- Salt and pepper, to taste
- Pinch of nutmeg (optional)
- Fresh parsley or chives, chopped, for garnish

Instructions:

1. Sauté Aromatics:
    - In a large pot, melt the butter over medium heat. Add the chopped onion and sauté for about 5 minutes until it is soft and translucent.
    - Add the minced garlic and cook for another 1-2 minutes until fragrant.
2. Cook Broccoli and Potato:
    - Add the fresh broccoli florets and diced potato to the pot. Pour in the vegetable or chicken broth.
    - Bring the mixture to a boil, then reduce the heat to low. Cover and simmer for about 20 minutes, or until the broccoli and potatoes are tender.
3. Blend the Soup:
    - Use an immersion blender to puree the soup until smooth. Alternatively, you can transfer the soup in batches to a countertop blender and blend until smooth, then return it to the pot.
4. Add Cream and Season:
    - Stir in the heavy cream. Heat the soup gently over low heat until warmed through. Do not let it boil.
    - Season with salt, pepper, and a pinch of nutmeg if desired. Adjust the seasoning to taste.
5. Serve:
    - Ladle the cream of broccoli soup into bowls. Garnish with chopped fresh parsley or chives.
6. Enjoy:
    - Serve hot with a side of crusty bread or a sprinkle of grated cheese if you like.

This creamy broccoli soup is rich and flavorful, making it a perfect choice for a cozy meal. The blend of tender broccoli, smooth potato, and creamy broth creates a delicious and satisfying dish. Enjoy your homemade cream of broccoli soup!

Fish Chowder

Ingredients:

- 2 tablespoons butter
- 1 onion, finely chopped
- 2 celery stalks, finely chopped
- 2 carrots, peeled and diced
- 3 cloves garlic, minced
- 1/4 cup all-purpose flour
- 4 cups fish stock or chicken broth
- 1 cup water
- 3 large potatoes, peeled and diced
- 1 bay leaf
- 1 teaspoon dried thyme
- Salt and pepper, to taste
- 1 1/2 pounds firm white fish fillets (such as cod, haddock, or halibut), cut into bite-sized pieces
- 1 cup heavy cream
- Fresh parsley or chives, chopped, for garnish

Instructions:

1. Sauté Vegetables:
    - In a large pot, melt the butter over medium heat. Add the chopped onion, celery, and carrots. Sauté for about 5 minutes until the vegetables are softened.
    - Add the minced garlic and cook for another 1-2 minutes until fragrant.
2. Make the Roux:
    - Sprinkle the flour over the vegetables and stir well to combine. Cook for about 2 minutes, stirring constantly, to eliminate the raw flour taste.
3. Add Broth and Potatoes:
    - Gradually add the fish stock or chicken broth and water, stirring constantly to avoid lumps. Add the diced potatoes, bay leaf, and dried thyme.
    - Bring the mixture to a boil, then reduce the heat to low. Cover and simmer for about 15-20 minutes, or until the potatoes are tender.
4. Add Fish:
    - Add the bite-sized fish pieces to the pot. Simmer gently for about 5-7 minutes, or until the fish is cooked through and opaque.
5. Add Cream and Season:
    - Stir in the heavy cream and heat the chowder gently over low heat until warmed through. Do not let it boil.
    - Season with salt and pepper to taste.
6. Serve:
    - Remove the bay leaf from the pot. Ladle the fish chowder into bowls. Garnish with chopped fresh parsley or chives.

7. Enjoy:
    - Serve hot with a side of crusty bread or oyster crackers.

This creamy fish chowder is rich and satisfying, with tender pieces of fish and a flavorful broth. It's a perfect dish for a cozy, comforting meal. Enjoy your homemade fish chowder!

Egg Drop Soup

Ingredients:

- 4 cups chicken broth
- 2 tablespoons cornstarch
- 1/4 teaspoon white pepper
- 1/2 teaspoon ground ginger
- 2 large eggs
- 1 egg yolk
- 1/2 cup frozen peas (optional)
- 1 green onion, thinly sliced
- 1 teaspoon soy sauce (optional)
- Salt, to taste
- Sesame oil, for drizzling (optional)

Instructions:

1. Prepare the Broth:
    - In a medium pot, bring the chicken broth to a boil. Reduce the heat to a simmer.
2. Thicken the Broth:
    - In a small bowl, mix the cornstarch with 1/4 cup of water to create a slurry. Stir the slurry into the simmering broth, continuing to stir until the broth thickens slightly.
3. Add Seasonings:
    - Add the white pepper and ground ginger to the pot. Stir to combine. If using, add soy sauce for additional flavor.
4. Prepare the Eggs:
    - In a small bowl, beat the eggs and the egg yolk together until well mixed.
5. Create the Egg Ribbons:
    - Slowly pour the beaten eggs into the simmering broth in a thin stream, stirring gently in a circular motion with a fork or a whisk to create the characteristic egg ribbons. The heat of the broth will cook the eggs almost instantly.
6. Add Peas and Green Onion:
    - If using, stir in the frozen peas and allow them to cook for 1-2 minutes until heated through.
    - Add the thinly sliced green onion to the soup.
7. Season to Taste:
    - Taste the soup and add salt as needed. Adjust the seasoning to your preference.
8. Serve:
    - Ladle the egg drop soup into bowls. Drizzle a few drops of sesame oil on top if desired.
9. Enjoy:
    - Serve hot, and enjoy your comforting bowl of homemade egg drop soup.

Egg Drop Soup is a quick and easy dish that delivers warmth and comfort with minimal ingredients. The delicate egg ribbons in a savory broth make it a perfect starter or light meal. Enjoy!

Vichyssoise (Cold Potato Leek Soup)

Ingredients:

- 3 tablespoons unsalted butter
- 3 leeks, white and light green parts only, thinly sliced
- 2 medium potatoes, peeled and diced
- 4 cups chicken or vegetable broth
- 1 cup heavy cream
- Salt and white pepper, to taste
- Chives, chopped, for garnish
- Optional: additional cream or yogurt for garnish

Instructions:

1. Sauté Leeks:
    - In a large pot, melt the butter over medium heat. Add the sliced leeks and sauté for about 5 minutes until they are soft and translucent.
2. Cook Potatoes:
    - Add the diced potatoes to the pot with the leeks. Pour in the chicken or vegetable broth, enough to cover the vegetables. Bring to a boil, then reduce the heat and simmer for about 20-25 minutes, or until the potatoes are tender and easily pierced with a fork.
3. Blend the Soup:
    - Remove the pot from the heat. Use an immersion blender to puree the soup until smooth and creamy. Alternatively, transfer the soup in batches to a countertop blender and blend until smooth, then return it to the pot.
4. Add Cream:
    - Stir in the heavy cream until well combined. Season with salt and white pepper to taste. Remember to taste and adjust the seasoning as needed.
5. Chill the Soup:
    - Cover the pot and refrigerate the soup until thoroughly chilled, at least 2 hours or overnight.
6. Serve:
    - Stir the soup before serving to ensure it's well mixed. Ladle the chilled Vichyssoise into bowls.
    - Garnish with chopped chives and a drizzle of additional cream or yogurt if desired.
7. Enjoy:
    - Serve cold as an elegant and refreshing starter for a summer meal.

Vichyssoise is a creamy and luxurious soup that highlights the natural sweetness of leeks and potatoes. Its silky texture and delicate flavor make it a delightful dish for warmer weather or any occasion where you want to impress with a sophisticated cold soup.

Sopa de Lima (Mexican Lime Soup)

Ingredients:

- 2 tablespoons vegetable oil
- 1 onion, finely chopped
- 2 cloves garlic, minced
- 2 tomatoes, diced
- 1 red bell pepper, diced
- 1 green bell pepper, diced
- 4 cups chicken broth
- 2 cups shredded cooked chicken
- 2 limes, juiced
- 2 teaspoons ground cumin
- 1 teaspoon dried oregano
- Salt and pepper, to taste
- Corn tortilla strips, for garnish
- Avocado slices, for garnish
- Fresh cilantro, chopped, for garnish

Instructions:

1. Sauté Aromatics:
    - In a large pot, heat the vegetable oil over medium heat. Add the finely chopped onion and sauté for about 5 minutes until it becomes translucent.
    - Add the minced garlic and cook for another minute until fragrant.
2. Add Vegetables:
    - Stir in the diced tomatoes, red bell pepper, and green bell pepper. Cook for about 5-7 minutes until the vegetables are softened.
3. Prepare the Broth:
    - Pour in the chicken broth and bring to a boil. Reduce the heat to low and simmer for about 10 minutes to allow the flavors to meld together.
4. Add Chicken and Seasonings:
    - Stir in the shredded cooked chicken, lime juice, ground cumin, and dried oregano. Season with salt and pepper to taste. Simmer for another 5 minutes to heat through.
5. Serve:
    - Ladle the Sopa de Lima into bowls. Garnish each bowl with corn tortilla strips, avocado slices, and chopped fresh cilantro.
6. Enjoy:
    - Serve hot and enjoy your flavorful and citrusy Mexican Lime Soup!

Sopa de Lima is a comforting and satisfying soup that combines the richness of chicken broth with the tangy brightness of lime juice and the robust flavors of vegetables and spices. It's perfect as a main dish or as a starter for a Mexican-inspired meal.

Cuban Black Bean Soup

Ingredients:

- 2 cups dried black beans, soaked overnight (or 4 cans black beans, drained and rinsed)
- 2 tablespoons olive oil
- 1 onion, chopped
- 1 green bell pepper, chopped
- 1 red bell pepper, chopped
- 4 cloves garlic, minced
- 2 teaspoons ground cumin
- 1 teaspoon dried oregano
- 1 bay leaf
- 1 tablespoon tomato paste
- 4 cups vegetable or chicken broth
- 2 cups water
- Salt and pepper, to taste
- Juice of 1 lime
- Optional toppings: chopped cilantro, diced red onion, sour cream or yogurt, avocado slices

Instructions:

1. Prepare the Beans (if using dried beans):
    - Drain and rinse the soaked black beans. In a large pot, cover the beans with water and bring to a boil. Reduce heat, cover, and simmer for about 1 to 1.5 hours, or until the beans are tender. Drain and set aside.
2. Sauté Aromatics:
    - In a large pot or Dutch oven, heat olive oil over medium heat. Add chopped onion, green bell pepper, and red bell pepper. Sauté for about 5-7 minutes until vegetables are softened.
3. Add Garlic and Spices:
    - Add minced garlic, ground cumin, dried oregano, bay leaf, and tomato paste. Stir well and cook for another 1-2 minutes until fragrant.
4. Simmer the Soup:
    - Add cooked black beans (or canned beans if using), vegetable or chicken broth, and water to the pot. Stir to combine. Bring the soup to a boil, then reduce heat to low. Cover and simmer for about 30-40 minutes to allow flavors to meld together. Stir occasionally.
5. Blend (Optional):
    - For a smoother consistency, use an immersion blender to partially blend the soup, leaving some beans intact for texture. Alternatively, blend a portion of the soup in a blender and return it to the pot.
6. Season and Serve:

- Season the soup with salt, pepper, and lime juice to taste. Adjust seasoning as needed.
7. Garnish and Serve:
    - Ladle the Cuban Black Bean Soup into bowls. Garnish with chopped cilantro, diced red onion, a dollop of sour cream or yogurt, and avocado slices if desired.
8. Enjoy:
    - Serve hot and enjoy this delicious and hearty Cuban-inspired soup!

Cuban Black Bean Soup is a comforting and flavorful dish that showcases the richness of black beans and the aromatic spices typical of Cuban cuisine. It's perfect for a satisfying meal any time of the year.

Sopa de Ajo (Spanish Garlic Soup)

Ingredients:

- 6 cups chicken broth
- 6 cloves garlic, thinly sliced
- 2 tablespoons olive oil
- 2 large eggs
- 1/4 cup dry white wine (optional)
- 1 teaspoon sweet paprika
- 1/2 teaspoon ground cumin
- Salt and pepper, to taste
- 2 cups day-old bread, cut into cubes
- Chopped fresh parsley, for garnish

Instructions:

1. Prepare the Broth:
    - In a large pot, heat the olive oil over medium heat. Add the thinly sliced garlic and sauté for 1-2 minutes until fragrant and just starting to turn golden.
2. Add Seasonings:
    - Stir in the sweet paprika and ground cumin. Cook for another minute, stirring constantly.
3. Simmer the Soup:
    - Pour in the chicken broth and bring to a simmer. Add the dry white wine, if using. Season with salt and pepper to taste.
4. Add Bread Cubes:
    - Add the bread cubes to the simmering soup. Stir well to combine.
5. Poach the Eggs:
    - Crack the eggs, one at a time, into a small bowl and gently slide them into the simmering soup. Poach the eggs for about 3-4 minutes, until the whites are set but the yolks are still runny.
6. Serve:
    - Ladle the Sopa de Ajo into bowls, making sure each serving has an egg. Garnish with chopped fresh parsley.
7. Enjoy:
    - Serve hot and enjoy the comforting flavors of garlic-infused broth and poached eggs with crusty bread.

Sopa de Ajo is a simple yet satisfying soup that highlights the bold flavors of garlic and paprika. It's perfect for a cozy meal, especially during cooler weather. Enjoy your homemade Spanish Garlic Soup!

Hot and Sour Soup

Ingredients:

- 4 cups chicken or vegetable broth
- 1/2 cup shiitake mushrooms, thinly sliced
- 1/2 cup firm tofu, diced into small cubes
- 2 tablespoons soy sauce
- 2 tablespoons rice vinegar (or to taste)
- 1 tablespoon cornstarch mixed with 2 tablespoons water
- 1 egg, beaten
- 1 teaspoon sesame oil
- 1/2 teaspoon ground white pepper (or to taste)
- Salt, to taste
- 2 green onions, thinly sliced
- Optional: bamboo shoots, wood ear mushrooms, or other vegetables

Instructions:

1. Prepare the Broth:
    - In a large pot, bring the chicken or vegetable broth to a boil.
2. Add Mushrooms and Tofu:
    - Add the thinly sliced shiitake mushrooms and diced tofu to the boiling broth. Reduce heat to medium and simmer for about 5 minutes, until the mushrooms are tender.
3. Season the Soup:
    - Stir in the soy sauce and rice vinegar. Adjust the amount of vinegar to achieve the desired level of tanginess.
    - Add the cornstarch mixture gradually while stirring constantly, until the soup slightly thickens.
4. Add Beaten Egg:
    - Slowly pour the beaten egg into the simmering soup in a thin stream, stirring gently with a fork or chopsticks to create silky egg ribbons.
5. Finish the Soup:
    - Add sesame oil and ground white pepper. Taste the soup and adjust seasoning with salt if needed.
6. Serve:
    - Ladle the Hot and Sour Soup into bowls. Garnish with thinly sliced green onions.
7. Enjoy:
    - Serve hot and enjoy the spicy, tangy flavors of this classic Chinese soup!

Hot and Sour Soup is a comforting and satisfying dish that can be customized with additional vegetables or protein according to personal preference. It's perfect as a starter or a light meal on its own.

New England Clam Chowder

Ingredients:

- 6 slices bacon, diced
- 1 onion, diced
- 2 celery stalks, diced
- 2 tablespoons unsalted butter
- 3 tablespoons all-purpose flour
- 3 cups chicken broth or clam juice
- 2 cups milk (whole milk or half-and-half)
- 1 bay leaf
- 1/2 teaspoon dried thyme
- 1/2 teaspoon ground black pepper
- 3 cups diced potatoes (about 2 large potatoes)
- 2 cups chopped clams, fresh or canned (drained)
- Salt, to taste
- Fresh parsley, chopped, for garnish
- Oyster crackers or crusty bread, for serving

Instructions:

1. Cook the Bacon:
    - In a large pot or Dutch oven, cook the diced bacon over medium heat until crispy. Remove bacon with a slotted spoon and set aside, leaving the bacon drippings in the pot.
2. Sauté Vegetables:
    - Add diced onion and celery to the pot with the bacon drippings. Sauté for about 5-7 minutes until softened.
3. Make the Roux:
    - Add butter to the pot and melt it with the vegetables. Stir in the flour to form a roux. Cook for 1-2 minutes, stirring constantly.
4. Simmer the Chowder:
    - Gradually whisk in the chicken broth or clam juice and milk, whisking constantly to prevent lumps. Add the bay leaf, dried thyme, and ground black pepper.
    - Stir in the diced potatoes. Bring the mixture to a boil, then reduce heat to low and simmer for about 15-20 minutes, or until the potatoes are tender and cooked through.
5. Add Clams:
    - Stir in the chopped clams and cooked bacon. Simmer for another 5 minutes until the clams are heated through. Taste and season with salt if needed.
6. Serve:
    - Remove the bay leaf from the chowder. Ladle the New England Clam Chowder into bowls. Garnish with chopped fresh parsley.
7. Enjoy:

- Serve hot, accompanied by oyster crackers or crusty bread.

New England Clam Chowder is a comforting and flavorful soup, perfect for cold days or anytime you crave a creamy seafood dish. It's a classic American favorite that's sure to warm you up!

Creamy Cauliflower Soup

Ingredients:

- 1 head cauliflower, chopped into florets
- 1 onion, chopped
- 2 cloves garlic, minced
- 2 tablespoons butter or olive oil
- 4 cups vegetable or chicken broth
- 1 cup milk or cream (or substitute with almond milk for a dairy-free option)
- Salt and pepper, to taste
- Pinch of nutmeg (optional)
- Fresh parsley or chives, chopped, for garnish

Instructions:

1. Sauté Vegetables:
    - In a large pot or Dutch oven, heat the butter or olive oil over medium heat. Add the chopped onion and sauté for 5-7 minutes until softened.
    - Add the minced garlic and cook for another minute until fragrant.
2. Cook Cauliflower:
    - Add the cauliflower florets to the pot. Pour in the vegetable or chicken broth until the cauliflower is just covered. Bring to a boil, then reduce heat to medium-low and simmer for about 15-20 minutes, or until the cauliflower is tender and easily pierced with a fork.
3. Blend the Soup:
    - Use an immersion blender to puree the soup until smooth and creamy. Alternatively, transfer the soup in batches to a countertop blender and blend until smooth, then return it to the pot.
4. Add Milk/Cream and Seasonings:
    - Stir in the milk or cream (or almond milk). Season with salt, pepper, and a pinch of nutmeg if desired. Adjust seasoning to taste.
5. Heat Through:
    - Heat the soup gently over low heat until warmed through. Do not boil once the dairy or alternative milk has been added.
6. Serve:
    - Ladle the creamy cauliflower soup into bowls. Garnish with chopped fresh parsley or chives.
7. Enjoy:
    - Serve hot and enjoy your creamy cauliflower soup as a comforting and nutritious meal.

This creamy cauliflower soup is versatile and can be adapted with additional spices or herbs according to your taste preferences. It's perfect for a cozy meal on a chilly day or as a starter for a larger meal.

Jamaican Chicken Soup

Ingredients:

- 1 whole chicken (about 3-4 lbs), cut into pieces
- 2 tablespoons vegetable oil
- 1 onion, chopped
- 3 cloves garlic, minced
- 2 carrots, peeled and diced
- 2 stalks celery, diced
- 1 bell pepper (any color), diced
- 2 potatoes, peeled and diced
- 1 scotch bonnet pepper (whole, for flavor, optional)
- 1 teaspoon dried thyme (or 2-3 sprigs fresh thyme)
- 1 teaspoon ground allspice
- 1 teaspoon ground turmeric
- Salt and pepper, to taste
- 8 cups chicken broth or water
- 1 cup coconut milk (optional, for added richness)
- Juice of 1 lime or lemon
- Fresh parsley or cilantro, chopped, for garnish

Instructions:

1. Brown the Chicken:
    - Heat vegetable oil in a large pot or Dutch oven over medium-high heat. Season the chicken pieces with salt and pepper, then brown them in batches until golden on all sides. Remove and set aside.
2. Sauté Aromatics:
    - In the same pot, add chopped onion, minced garlic, carrots, celery, and bell pepper. Sauté for about 5-7 minutes until the vegetables begin to soften.
3. Add Spices and Herbs:
    - Stir in dried thyme, ground allspice, and ground turmeric. Cook for another minute until fragrant.
4. Simmer the Soup:
    - Return the browned chicken pieces to the pot. Add potatoes and scotch bonnet pepper (if using). Pour in chicken broth or water, ensuring the chicken and vegetables are covered. Bring to a boil, then reduce heat to low. Cover and simmer for about 30-40 minutes, or until the chicken is cooked through and tender.
5. Finish the Soup:
    - Remove the scotch bonnet pepper (if using). Stir in coconut milk (if using) and lime or lemon juice. Taste and adjust seasoning with salt and pepper as needed.
6. Serve:

- Ladle the Jamaican Chicken Soup into bowls. Garnish with chopped fresh parsley or cilantro.
7. Enjoy:
    - Serve hot and enjoy the delicious flavors of this Jamaican-inspired chicken soup!

Jamaican Chicken Soup is often served with slices of bread, dumplings, or rice on the side. It's a comforting and satisfying meal that showcases the vibrant flavors of Caribbean cuisine.

Mushroom Barley Soup

Ingredients:

- 1 cup pearl barley
- 8 cups vegetable or beef broth
- 2 tablespoons olive oil or butter
- 1 onion, chopped
- 2 carrots, diced
- 2 celery stalks, diced
- 3 cloves garlic, minced
- 1 lb mushrooms (such as cremini or button), sliced
- 1 teaspoon dried thyme
- 1 bay leaf
- Salt and pepper, to taste
- Fresh parsley, chopped, for garnish

Instructions:

1. Cook the Barley:
   - Rinse the pearl barley under cold water. In a medium pot, bring 3 cups of water to a boil. Add the rinsed barley, reduce heat to low, cover, and simmer for about 30-40 minutes, or until barley is tender. Drain any excess water and set aside.
2. Sauté Vegetables:
   - In a large pot or Dutch oven, heat olive oil or butter over medium heat. Add chopped onion, diced carrots, and diced celery. Sauté for about 5-7 minutes until vegetables start to soften.
3. Cook Mushrooms:
   - Add minced garlic and sliced mushrooms to the pot. Cook for another 5-7 minutes until mushrooms are browned and softened.
4. Simmer the Soup:
   - Pour in vegetable or beef broth and bring to a boil. Add cooked barley, dried thyme, and bay leaf. Season with salt and pepper to taste.
   - Reduce heat to low, cover, and simmer for about 20-25 minutes to allow flavors to meld together.
5. Adjust Seasoning and Serve:
   - Taste the soup and adjust seasoning if needed. Remove the bay leaf before serving.
   - Ladle Mushroom Barley Soup into bowls. Garnish with chopped fresh parsley.
6. Enjoy:
   - Serve hot and enjoy this hearty and flavorful Mushroom Barley Soup!

This soup can be made ahead and reheated, making it a great option for meal prep or for a comforting meal on a chilly day. It's a satisfying dish that combines the nuttiness of barley with the savory richness of mushrooms and vegetables.

Turkey Chili Soup

Ingredients:

- 1 tablespoon olive oil
- 1 onion, diced
- 3 cloves garlic, minced
- 1 red bell pepper, diced
- 1 green bell pepper, diced
- 1 jalapeño pepper, seeded and diced (optional, for heat)
- 1 lb ground turkey (preferably lean)
- 2 tablespoons chili powder
- 1 teaspoon ground cumin
- 1/2 teaspoon paprika
- 1/2 teaspoon dried oregano
- 1/4 teaspoon cayenne pepper (optional, for extra heat)
- Salt and pepper, to taste
- 1 (15 oz) can diced tomatoes
- 1 (15 oz) can tomato sauce
- 3 cups low-sodium chicken broth
- 1 (15 oz) can black beans, drained and rinsed
- 1 cup frozen corn kernels
- Juice of 1 lime
- Fresh cilantro, chopped, for garnish
- Shredded cheese, sour cream, avocado slices, tortilla chips (optional, for serving)

Instructions:

1. Sauté Aromatics:
    - Heat olive oil in a large pot or Dutch oven over medium heat. Add diced onion, minced garlic, diced red bell pepper, diced green bell pepper, and diced jalapeño (if using). Sauté for 5-7 minutes until vegetables are softened.
2. Brown Turkey:
    - Add ground turkey to the pot. Break it up with a spoon and cook until browned and cooked through, about 5-7 minutes.
3. Season the Soup:
    - Stir in chili powder, ground cumin, paprika, dried oregano, cayenne pepper (if using), salt, and pepper. Cook for 1-2 minutes until spices are fragrant.
4. Add Tomatoes and Broth:
    - Add diced tomatoes (with juices), tomato sauce, and chicken broth to the pot. Stir well to combine.
5. Simmer the Soup:
    - Bring the soup to a boil, then reduce heat to low. Cover and simmer for 20-25 minutes, stirring occasionally.
6. Add Beans and Corn:

- Stir in black beans and frozen corn kernels. Simmer for an additional 5-10 minutes until heated through.
7. **Finish and Serve:**
    - Stir in lime juice. Taste and adjust seasoning with salt and pepper if needed.
    - Ladle Turkey Chili Soup into bowls. Garnish with chopped fresh cilantro.
    - Serve hot, and optionally garnish with shredded cheese, a dollop of sour cream, avocado slices, and tortilla chips.
8. **Enjoy:**
    - Enjoy this flavorful and hearty Turkey Chili Soup as a comforting meal!

This soup is packed with protein and vegetables, making it a nutritious and filling option for lunch or dinner. It's also great for leftovers and can be frozen for future meals.

Creamy Tomato Tortellini Soup

Ingredients:

- 1 tablespoon olive oil
- 1 onion, finely chopped
- 3 cloves garlic, minced
- 1 teaspoon dried basil
- 1 teaspoon dried oregano
- 1/2 teaspoon dried thyme
- 1/4 teaspoon red pepper flakes (optional, for heat)
- 1 (28 oz) can crushed tomatoes
- 4 cups vegetable or chicken broth
- 1 cup heavy cream (or half-and-half for a lighter option)
- 1 tablespoon tomato paste
- Salt and pepper, to taste
- 1 lb fresh or frozen cheese tortellini
- Fresh basil, chopped, for garnish
- Grated Parmesan cheese, for garnish

Instructions:

1. Sauté Aromatics:
    - In a large pot or Dutch oven, heat olive oil over medium heat. Add finely chopped onion and sauté for 5-7 minutes until softened.
2. Add Garlic and Spices:
    - Add minced garlic, dried basil, dried oregano, dried thyme, and red pepper flakes (if using). Cook for 1-2 minutes until fragrant.
3. Simmer Tomato Base:
    - Stir in crushed tomatoes, vegetable or chicken broth, heavy cream, and tomato paste. Season with salt and pepper to taste. Bring to a simmer.
4. Cook Tortellini:
    - Add fresh or frozen cheese tortellini to the simmering soup. Cook according to package instructions until tortellini are tender, usually about 7-10 minutes.
5. Finish and Serve:
    - Once tortellini are cooked, taste and adjust seasoning if needed.
    - Ladle Creamy Tomato Tortellini Soup into bowls. Garnish with chopped fresh basil and grated Parmesan cheese.
6. Enjoy:
    - Serve hot and enjoy the creamy and comforting flavors of this Tomato Tortellini Soup!

This soup is perfect for a cozy meal during colder months and pairs well with crusty bread or a side salad. It's creamy, tomato-rich, and filled with cheesy tortellini goodness.

Cabbage Soup

Ingredients:

- 1 tablespoon olive oil or vegetable oil
- 1 onion, diced
- 3 cloves garlic, minced
- 4 cups vegetable or chicken broth
- 1 medium head of cabbage, chopped (about 6-8 cups)
- 2 carrots, diced
- 2 celery stalks, diced
- 1 (15 oz) can diced tomatoes (with juices)
- 1 teaspoon dried thyme
- 1 teaspoon paprika
- Salt and pepper, to taste
- Optional: 1 cup cooked beans (such as kidney beans or white beans)
- Fresh parsley, chopped, for garnish

Instructions:

1. Sauté Aromatics:
    - Heat olive oil in a large pot or Dutch oven over medium heat. Add diced onion and sauté for 5-7 minutes until softened.
    - Add minced garlic and sauté for another minute until fragrant.
2. Add Vegetables and Herbs:
    - Stir in chopped cabbage, diced carrots, and diced celery. Cook for about 5 minutes, stirring occasionally, until vegetables start to soften.
3. Simmer the Soup:
    - Pour in vegetable or chicken broth and add diced tomatoes (with juices). Stir in dried thyme, paprika, salt, and pepper.
    - Bring the soup to a boil, then reduce heat to low. Cover and simmer for 20-25 minutes, or until vegetables are tender.
4. Add Beans (if using) and Adjust Seasoning:
    - If using cooked beans, add them to the soup during the last 5 minutes of cooking to heat through.
    - Taste the soup and adjust seasoning with salt and pepper if needed.
5. Serve:
    - Ladle Cabbage Soup into bowls. Garnish with chopped fresh parsley.
6. Enjoy:
    - Serve hot and enjoy this simple and nourishing Cabbage Soup as a comforting meal.

Cabbage soup is versatile and can be customized with additional vegetables or herbs according to your preferences. It's a healthy option that's low in calories and high in fiber, making it great for a light lunch or dinner.

Malaysian Laksa Soup

Ingredients:

For the Laksa Paste:

- 2 stalks lemongrass, white part only, chopped
- 4-5 shallots, chopped
- 4 cloves garlic, chopped
- 1-inch piece of ginger, peeled and chopped
- 2 tablespoons chili paste or 2-3 fresh red chilies, chopped
- 1 tablespoon ground coriander
- 1 teaspoon ground cumin
- 1 teaspoon ground turmeric
- 1 tablespoon vegetable oil

For the Soup:

- 4 cups chicken or vegetable broth
- 1 (14 oz) can coconut milk
- 1 tablespoon fish sauce (optional, for extra umami)
- 1 tablespoon brown sugar or palm sugar
- Salt, to taste
- 1 lb shrimp, chicken, or tofu, sliced
- 8 oz rice vermicelli noodles or egg noodles
- Bean sprouts, lime wedges, chopped cilantro, chopped green onions, for garnish

Instructions:

1. Make the Laksa Paste:
    - In a food processor or blender, combine lemongrass, shallots, garlic, ginger, chili paste (or fresh chilies), ground coriander, ground cumin, and ground turmeric. Blend until a smooth paste forms.
2. Cook the Laksa Paste:
    - Heat vegetable oil in a large pot over medium heat. Add the Laksa paste and cook for 5-7 minutes, stirring constantly, until fragrant.
3. Prepare the Broth:
    - Pour in chicken or vegetable broth and coconut milk. Stir well to combine. Add fish sauce (if using), brown sugar or palm sugar, and salt to taste. Bring to a simmer.
4. Add Protein and Noodles:
    - Add sliced shrimp, chicken, or tofu to the simmering broth. Cook until protein is cooked through, about 5 minutes for shrimp or tofu, or 10 minutes for chicken.
    - Meanwhile, cook rice vermicelli noodles or egg noodles according to package instructions. Drain and set aside.

5. Assemble Laksa Soup:
    - Divide cooked noodles among serving bowls. Ladle the hot Laksa broth over the noodles and protein.
    - Garnish with bean sprouts, lime wedges, chopped cilantro, and chopped green onions.
6. Serve:
    - Serve immediately and enjoy the aromatic and flavorful Malaysian Laksa Soup!

Laksa is a versatile dish, and you can adjust the spiciness by adding more or less chili paste or chilies. This recipe offers a balanced blend of spices and coconut milk, creating a satisfying soup that's perfect for a comforting meal.

Escarole Soup

Ingredients:

For the Meatballs:

- 1/2 lb ground pork or ground turkey
- 1/2 lb ground beef
- 1/2 cup breadcrumbs
- 1/4 cup grated Parmesan cheese
- 1 egg
- 2 cloves garlic, minced
- 1 teaspoon dried oregano
- 1 teaspoon dried basil
- Salt and pepper, to taste

For the Soup:

- 1 tablespoon olive oil
- 1 onion, diced
- 2 carrots, diced
- 2 celery stalks, diced
- 2 cloves garlic, minced
- 8 cups chicken broth
- 1 head escarole, chopped (about 6-8 cups)
- 1 cup small pasta (such as acini di pepe or orzo)
- Salt and pepper, to taste
- Fresh parsley, chopped, for garnish
- Grated Parmesan cheese, for serving

Instructions:

1. Make the Meatballs:
    - In a bowl, combine ground pork or turkey, ground beef, breadcrumbs, grated Parmesan cheese, egg, minced garlic, dried oregano, dried basil, salt, and pepper. Mix until well combined.
    - Form mixture into small meatballs, about 1-inch in diameter.
2. Cook the Meatballs:
    - Heat olive oil in a large pot or Dutch oven over medium heat. Add meatballs in batches and cook until browned on all sides, about 5-7 minutes. Remove meatballs and set aside.
3. Sauté Vegetables:
    - In the same pot, add diced onion, diced carrots, and diced celery. Sauté for 5-7 minutes until vegetables are softened. Add minced garlic and cook for another minute until fragrant.

4. Simmer the Soup:
    - Pour in chicken broth and bring to a boil. Add chopped escarole and small pasta (such as acini di pepe or orzo). Reduce heat to medium-low and simmer for about 10 minutes, or until pasta is tender and cooked through.
5. Add Meatballs and Season:
    - Return the cooked meatballs to the pot. Simmer for an additional 5 minutes to heat through. Season with salt and pepper to taste.
6. Serve:
    - Ladle Escarole Soup into bowls. Garnish with chopped fresh parsley and grated Parmesan cheese.
7. Enjoy:
    - Serve hot and enjoy this comforting and flavorful Escarole Soup!

Escarole Soup is hearty and nutritious, perfect for a cozy meal during colder months. The combination of meatballs, vegetables, and escarole in a savory broth makes it a satisfying dish that's also versatile and easy to customize according to your preferences.

Irish Potato Soup

Ingredients:

- 2 tablespoons butter
- 1 onion, chopped
- 2 leeks, white and light green parts only, chopped
- 3 cloves garlic, minced
- 4 cups potatoes, peeled and diced (about 4 medium potatoes)
- 4 cups vegetable or chicken broth
- 1 cup milk or cream
- Salt and pepper, to taste
- Fresh chives or parsley, chopped, for garnish
- Optional: grated cheddar cheese, crispy bacon bits, sour cream

Instructions:

1. Sauté Aromatics:
    - In a large pot or Dutch oven, melt butter over medium heat. Add chopped onion and leeks. Sauté for 5-7 minutes until softened.
2. Add Potatoes and Garlic:
    - Add minced garlic and diced potatoes to the pot. Stir and cook for another 1-2 minutes.
3. Simmer the Soup:
    - Pour in vegetable or chicken broth, enough to cover the potatoes. Bring to a boil, then reduce heat to medium-low. Cover and simmer for about 15-20 minutes, or until potatoes are tender and easily pierced with a fork.
4. Blend the Soup:
    - Use an immersion blender to puree the soup until smooth and creamy. Alternatively, carefully transfer the soup in batches to a countertop blender and blend until smooth. Be cautious with hot liquids.
5. Add Milk or Cream:
    - Stir in milk or cream to achieve desired consistency and creaminess. Heat through gently over low heat. Season with salt and pepper to taste.
6. Serve:
    - Ladle Irish Potato Soup into bowls. Garnish with chopped fresh chives or parsley.
7. Optional Garnishes:
    - If desired, top each bowl with grated cheddar cheese, crispy bacon bits, and a dollop of sour cream.
8. Enjoy:
    - Serve hot and enjoy this creamy and comforting Irish Potato Soup!

This soup is versatile and can be adapted with additional herbs or spices according to your taste preferences. It's perfect served with crusty bread or as a starter for a larger meal.

Swiss Chard Soup

Ingredients:

- 1 tablespoon olive oil
- 1 onion, chopped
- 3 cloves garlic, minced
- 2 carrots, diced
- 2 celery stalks, diced
- 1 potato, peeled and diced
- 6 cups vegetable broth
- 1 bunch Swiss chard, stems removed and leaves chopped
- 1 (15 oz) can white beans (such as cannellini beans), drained and rinsed
- 1 teaspoon dried thyme
- Salt and pepper, to taste
- Fresh lemon juice, to taste
- Grated Parmesan cheese, for garnish (optional)

Instructions:

1. Sauté Aromatics:
    - Heat olive oil in a large pot or Dutch oven over medium heat. Add chopped onion and sauté for 5-7 minutes until softened.
    - Add minced garlic and cook for another minute until fragrant.
2. Add Vegetables and Broth:
    - Stir in diced carrots, diced celery, and diced potato. Cook for 5 minutes, stirring occasionally.
    - Pour in vegetable broth and bring to a boil.
3. Simmer the Soup:
    - Reduce heat to medium-low. Add chopped Swiss chard leaves and drained white beans to the pot. Stir in dried thyme, salt, and pepper to taste.
    - Cover and simmer for about 15-20 minutes, or until vegetables are tender.
4. Finish and Serve:
    - Remove the pot from heat. Taste the soup and adjust seasoning if needed. Add fresh lemon juice to brighten the flavors.
    - Ladle Swiss Chard Soup into bowls. Garnish with grated Parmesan cheese, if desired.
5. Enjoy:
    - Serve hot and enjoy this hearty and nutritious Swiss Chard Soup!

This soup is packed with vegetables and beans, making it a wholesome meal on its own. It's also versatile and can be customized with additional herbs or spices according to your preferences. Enjoy it with crusty bread for a complete and satisfying meal.

Chicken and Rice Soup

Ingredients:

- 1 tablespoon olive oil
- 1 onion, diced
- 2 carrots, diced
- 2 celery stalks, diced
- 3 cloves garlic, minced
- 1 teaspoon dried thyme
- 1 teaspoon dried parsley
- 1 bay leaf
- Salt and pepper, to taste
- 6 cups chicken broth
- 1 cup long-grain white rice
- 2 cups cooked chicken, shredded or diced (from rotisserie chicken or cooked chicken breasts)
- Fresh parsley, chopped, for garnish
- Lemon wedges, for serving (optional)

Instructions:

1. Sauté Aromatics:
    - Heat olive oil in a large pot or Dutch oven over medium heat. Add diced onion, diced carrots, and diced celery. Sauté for 5-7 minutes until vegetables are softened.
2. Add Garlic and Herbs:
    - Add minced garlic, dried thyme, dried parsley, bay leaf, salt, and pepper. Cook for another minute until fragrant.
3. Simmer the Soup:
    - Pour in chicken broth and bring to a boil. Stir in white rice and reduce heat to medium-low. Cover and simmer for 15-20 minutes, or until rice is tender.
4. Add Chicken:
    - Stir in cooked chicken and simmer for another 5 minutes to heat through.
5. Adjust Seasoning and Serve:
    - Taste the soup and adjust seasoning with salt and pepper if needed. Remove the bay leaf before serving.
6. Garnish and Serve:
    - Ladle Chicken and Rice Soup into bowls. Garnish with chopped fresh parsley.
    - Serve hot, optionally with lemon wedges for squeezing over the soup.
7. Enjoy:
    - Enjoy this comforting Chicken and Rice Soup as a hearty meal on its own or with a side of crusty bread.

This soup is perfect for using leftover chicken and can be easily customized by adding additional vegetables or herbs according to your taste. It's a comforting dish that's great for warming up on a chilly day.

Chicken Mulligatawny Soup

Ingredients:

- 1 tablespoon vegetable oil
- 1 onion, finely chopped
- 2 carrots, diced
- 2 celery stalks, diced
- 3 cloves garlic, minced
- 1 tablespoon fresh ginger, minced
- 1 tablespoon curry powder
- 1 teaspoon ground cumin
- 1 teaspoon ground coriander
- 1/2 teaspoon turmeric powder
- 1/4 teaspoon cayenne pepper (adjust to taste)
- 1 lb boneless, skinless chicken breast or thighs, diced
- 4 cups chicken broth
- 1 cup coconut milk (full-fat for creaminess)
- 1 cup diced tomatoes (canned or fresh)
- 1/2 cup red lentils (optional, for added texture and protein)
- Salt and pepper, to taste
- Fresh cilantro, chopped, for garnish
- Cooked rice or naan bread, for serving

Instructions:

1. Sauté Aromatics:
    - Heat vegetable oil in a large pot or Dutch oven over medium heat. Add chopped onion, diced carrots, and diced celery. Sauté for 5-7 minutes until vegetables are softened.
2. Add Spices:
    - Add minced garlic, minced ginger, curry powder, ground cumin, ground coriander, turmeric powder, and cayenne pepper. Stir well and cook for 1-2 minutes until fragrant.
3. Cook Chicken:
    - Add diced chicken to the pot. Cook for 5-7 minutes, stirring occasionally, until chicken is browned on all sides.
4. Simmer Soup:
    - Pour in chicken broth, coconut milk, diced tomatoes, and red lentils (if using). Stir well to combine. Bring to a boil, then reduce heat to medium-low. Cover and simmer for 20-25 minutes, or until lentils are tender and chicken is cooked through.
5. Adjust Seasoning:
    - Taste the soup and season with salt and pepper as needed.
6. Serve:

- Ladle Chicken Mulligatawny Soup into bowls. Garnish with chopped fresh cilantro.
- Serve hot, optionally with cooked rice or naan bread on the side.

7. Enjoy:
    - Enjoy this flavorful and aromatic Chicken Mulligatawny Soup as a satisfying meal!

This soup is rich in flavor from the spices and creamy coconut milk, with tender chunks of chicken and hearty vegetables. It's perfect for a comforting dinner or lunch, especially on cooler days.

Japanese Clear Soup

Ingredients:

- 6 cups dashi stock (Japanese fish broth, can be made with kombu and bonito flakes or using dashi powder)
- 1/2 cup mirin (Japanese sweet rice wine)
- 1/4 cup soy sauce
- 1 teaspoon salt
- 1 block firm tofu, diced into small cubes
- 1 cup sliced mushrooms (shiitake, enoki, or your choice)
- 1/2 cup sliced bamboo shoots (canned or fresh)
- 1 green onion, thinly sliced (for garnish)
- Fresh cilantro or parsley, chopped (optional, for garnish)

Instructions:

1. Prepare Dashi Stock:
   - If making dashi from scratch, soak a piece of kombu (dried kelp) in 6 cups of water overnight. Then, bring it to a boil and remove the kombu just before it boils to prevent bitterness. Add bonito flakes and allow it to steep for 5 minutes before straining.
2. Season the Broth:
   - In a large pot, combine dashi stock, mirin, soy sauce, and salt. Bring to a gentle simmer over medium heat.
3. Add Tofu and Vegetables:
   - Add diced tofu, sliced mushrooms, and sliced bamboo shoots to the simmering broth. Cook for about 3-4 minutes, or until tofu is heated through and vegetables are tender.
4. Serve:
   - Ladle Japanese Clear Soup into bowls. Garnish with thinly sliced green onions and chopped cilantro or parsley, if using.
5. Enjoy:
   - Serve hot as a light and refreshing starter or alongside a Japanese meal. Enjoy the delicate flavors of this traditional Japanese Clear Soup!

Japanese Clear Soup is known for its simplicity and clean taste, making it a perfect complement to richer or more flavorful dishes in a Japanese meal. Adjust the seasoning according to your taste preferences, and feel free to customize with your favorite vegetables or tofu variations.

Corn and Crab Chowder

Ingredients:

- 4 tablespoons unsalted butter
- 1 onion, diced
- 2 celery stalks, diced
- 1 red bell pepper, diced
- 3 cloves garlic, minced
- 1/4 cup all-purpose flour
- 4 cups chicken or vegetable broth
- 3 cups fresh or frozen corn kernels (about 4-5 ears of corn)
- 1 lb lump crab meat, picked over for shells
- 2 cups half-and-half or heavy cream
- 1 teaspoon Old Bay seasoning (or to taste)
- Salt and pepper, to taste
- Fresh parsley, chopped, for garnish
- Crispy cooked bacon, crumbled (optional, for garnish)

Instructions:

1. Sauté Vegetables:
    - In a large pot or Dutch oven, melt butter over medium heat. Add diced onion, diced celery, and diced red bell pepper. Sauté for 5-7 minutes until vegetables are softened.
2. Add Garlic and Flour:
    - Add minced garlic to the pot and cook for another minute until fragrant. Sprinkle flour over the vegetables and stir to coat evenly. Cook for 2-3 minutes to cook off the raw flour taste.
3. Simmer the Chowder:
    - Gradually pour in chicken or vegetable broth, stirring constantly to prevent lumps. Bring to a boil, then reduce heat to medium-low.
4. Add Corn and Crab:
    - Stir in fresh or frozen corn kernels and lump crab meat. Simmer for about 10-15 minutes, stirring occasionally, until corn is tender and flavors are blended.
5. Add Cream and Seasoning:
    - Pour in half-and-half or heavy cream. Season with Old Bay seasoning, salt, and pepper to taste. Simmer for another 5 minutes, stirring occasionally, until heated through.
6. Serve:
    - Ladle Corn and Crab Chowder into bowls. Garnish with chopped fresh parsley and crumbled crispy bacon, if desired.
7. Enjoy:
    - Serve hot and enjoy this creamy and flavorful Corn and Crab Chowder as a delicious meal!

This chowder is perfect for showcasing the sweetness of corn and the delicate flavor of crab. It's hearty enough to serve as a main dish or as a starter for a larger meal. Pair it with crusty bread or oyster crackers for a complete and satisfying meal.

Portuguese Caldo Verde

Ingredients:

- 2 tablespoons olive oil
- 1 onion, finely chopped
- 3 cloves garlic, minced
- 4 potatoes, peeled and thinly sliced
- 6 cups chicken or vegetable broth
- 1 lb kale or collard greens, tough stems removed and leaves thinly sliced
- 8 oz chorizo or linguica sausage, sliced into thin rounds
- Salt and pepper, to taste
- Red wine vinegar, for serving (optional)

Instructions:

1. Sauté Aromatics:
    - Heat olive oil in a large pot or Dutch oven over medium heat. Add finely chopped onion and sauté for 5-7 minutes until softened.
    - Add minced garlic and cook for another minute until fragrant.
2. Add Potatoes and Broth:
    - Add thinly sliced potatoes to the pot. Pour in chicken or vegetable broth. Bring to a boil, then reduce heat to medium-low. Simmer for about 15-20 minutes, or until potatoes are tender.
3. Prepare Kale or Collard Greens:
    - While potatoes are cooking, prepare the kale or collard greens. Stack the leaves, roll them up, and thinly slice into ribbons.
4. Cook Sausage and Greens:
    - In a separate pan, cook chorizo or linguica sausage over medium heat until lightly browned and cooked through, about 5-7 minutes. Remove from pan and set aside.
    - Add sliced kale or collard greens to the pot with the potatoes. Simmer for 5-7 minutes, or until greens are tender and bright green.
5. Combine and Season:
    - Return cooked sausage to the pot. Season Caldo Verde with salt and pepper to taste. Stir well to combine and simmer for another 2-3 minutes to heat through.
6. Serve:
    - Ladle Caldo Verde into bowls. Serve hot, optionally drizzling with a splash of red wine vinegar for extra tang.
7. Enjoy:
    - Enjoy this comforting and hearty Portuguese Caldo Verde soup as a main dish or starter, accompanied by crusty bread.

Caldo Verde is a beloved dish in Portuguese cuisine, known for its comforting and satisfying qualities. It's perfect for chilly evenings and can be adapted with different types of sausage or greens according to your preference.

Hungarian Goulash Soup

Ingredients:

- 2 tablespoons vegetable oil
- 1 onion, finely chopped
- 2 cloves garlic, minced
- 1 lb beef stew meat, cut into bite-sized pieces
- 2 tablespoons Hungarian sweet paprika
- 1 teaspoon smoked paprika (optional, for extra flavor)
- 1 teaspoon caraway seeds
- 2 tomatoes, diced (or 1 (14 oz) can diced tomatoes)
- 2 potatoes, peeled and diced
- 2 carrots, peeled and diced
- 1 bell pepper, diced
- 4 cups beef broth
- 1 bay leaf
- Salt and pepper, to taste
- Chopped fresh parsley or dill, for garnish
- Sour cream, for serving (optional)

Instructions:

1. Sauté Aromatics:
    - Heat vegetable oil in a large pot or Dutch oven over medium heat. Add finely chopped onion and sauté for 5-7 minutes until softened.
    - Add minced garlic and cook for another minute until fragrant.
2. Brown Beef:
    - Add beef stew meat to the pot. Cook, stirring occasionally, until beef is browned on all sides.
3. Add Paprika and Spices:
    - Sprinkle Hungarian sweet paprika, smoked paprika (if using), and caraway seeds over the beef and onions. Stir well to coat the meat and onions with the spices.
4. Add Vegetables and Broth:
    - Add diced tomatoes, diced potatoes, diced carrots, and diced bell pepper to the pot. Pour in beef broth and add bay leaf. Stir to combine.
5. Simmer the Soup:
    - Bring the soup to a boil, then reduce heat to medium-low. Cover and simmer for about 1 to 1.5 hours, or until beef is tender and flavors are blended. Stir occasionally and check for desired tenderness of vegetables.
6. Adjust Seasoning:
    - Remove bay leaf from the soup. Season with salt and pepper to taste.
7. Serve:
    - Ladle Hungarian Goulash Soup into bowls. Garnish with chopped fresh parsley or dill.

- Serve hot, optionally with a dollop of sour cream on top.
8. Enjoy:
    - Enjoy this flavorful and comforting Hungarian Goulash Soup as a satisfying meal!

Hungarian Goulash Soup is often served with hearty bread or dumplings, and the addition of sour cream adds a creamy texture and richness to the soup. It's a classic dish that's perfect for warming up on colder days.

www.ingramcontent.com/pod-product-compliance
Lightning Source LLC
LaVergne TN
LVHW081616060526
838201LV00054B/2280